THE MAREVA INJUNCTION
AND RELATED ORDERS

THE MAREVA
INJUNCTION
AND RELATED ORDERS

By

MARK S. W. HOYLE
B.A. (Hons.), Ph.D., A.C.I.Arb.
of the Inner Temple and
Gray's Inn, Barrister

LONDON   NEW YORK   HAMBURG   HONG KONG
LLOYD'S OF LONDON PRESS LTD.
1985

Lloyd's of London Press Ltd.
Legal Publishing and Conferences Division
26–30 Artillery Lane, London E1 7LX

U.S.A. AND CANADA
Lloyd's of London Press Inc.
87 Terminal Drive, Plainview
New York, NY 10003 USA

GERMANY
Lloyd's of London Press
P O Box 11 23 47, Deichstrasse 41
2000 Hamburg 11, West Germany

SOUTH EAST ASIA
Lloyd's of London Press (Far East) Ltd.
1502 Chung Nam Building
1 Lockhart Road, Wanchai
Hong Kong

©
Mark S. W. Hoyle
1985

British Library Cataloguing in Publication Data
Hoyle, Mark S. W.
   The Mareva injunction and related orders.
   1. Debtor and creditor—England
   2. Injunctions—England
   I. Title
   344.206'77   KD1740

ISBN 1–85044–044–1

Typeset in Century by Wessex Typesetters, Frome, Somerset
Printed in Great Britain by Billings & Sons Limited, Worcester

Foreword

For many years practitioners, particularly those familiar with continental systems of law, were aware that the absence of any general remedy to prevent debtors from evading liability by salting away their assets constituted a serious weakness in the common law and resulted, from time to time, in irremediable injustice. Some of us expected, even pressed for, legislative reform to fill this gap in our legal armoury. Then, quite suddenly and (to me at least) unexpectedly, the courts took action. In two historic decisions in 1975, the Court of Appeal extended the law of injunctions and so provided the remedy which was so badly needed; it is from the second of those cases that the *Mareva* injunction has derived its name.

Over 10 years have passed since that creative development. During that period, we have seen the principles underlying the *Mareva* injunction gradually worked out from case to case. This essentially English pragmatic approach has much to commend it, since it ensures that legal development is founded upon reaction to fact-situations rather than derived from preconceived theories. As a result, we have a substantial body of case law to guide the practitioner in his work.

Mr Hoyle, and his publishers, have rightly judged that the time is now ripe for these various decisions to be gathered together, analysed and expounded in a book. I have read this book in page proof with great interest. I have no doubt that it will fill a great need and that it will be of very considerable assistance to practising lawyers. I feel honoured to be asked to provide a foreword to this book; and I am very happy to take the opportunity to commend it. I have no doubt that it will find a place on the bookshelves of many practitioners, and that it will be studied by them with interest and frequently consulted by them with profit in the course of their work.

SIR ROBERT GOFF
a Lord Justice of Appeal

Preface

The *Mareva* injunction is a powerful weapon in the arsenal available to legal practitioners. No observer of the law's development since 1975 can have failed to notice the impact the *Mareva* injunction has had (together with the Anton Piller order, and associated orders for discovery) on the resolution of disputes and the attitudes of plaintiffs and defendants. Many litigants and their professional advisers have been thankful for the protection the *Mareva* has offered.

This book is an attempt to set out both the background to the *Mareva* injunction, and its present and potential use, and thus hopefully to provide practitioners and others with a manageable guide to this powerful procedure, especially as its successful use relies almost entirely on the discretion of the judiciary, and on the day-to-day practice in the courts.

In some footnotes the date of judgment (as well as the usual citation) has been given to illustrate, on reading the text, the gradual and timely build-up of authority. "Unreported" cases are also referred to where they add to or underwrite a particular point. The law is basically stated as at January 1985, with later corrections as at the time of printing.

Many colleagues and friends have offered advice and helpful suggestions in the course of writing this work, and I would like to thank them; special thanks are due to Karen Garner, who was instrumental in forging my present interest in the *Mareva* injunction, and to Mr David Bird, the Commercial Court Listing Officer, who not only has had the task of administering most *Mareva* applications in recent years, but who has also provided me with much vital information.

I am also grateful to Philip Littler and Simon Gutteridge of Lloyd's of London Press, who suggested I might like to write this work. Their interest and assistance has been very valuable.

Finally, I must thank my wife for all her encouragement and support.

City of London   MSWH
March 1985

Contents

Table of Cases

Table of Legislation

CHAPTER 1

Introduction

The first cases

In May 1975, Japanese shipowners issued a writ against Greek charterers, claiming various sums of hire owing for three ships that had been chartered by the defendants. The plaintiffs feared that the charterers would take steps to remove their funds from the jurisdiction of the English courts, and so effectively negate any judgment eventually entered against them. Accordingly, four days after issue of the writ, the shipowners applied *ex parte* to the High Court for an interim injunction restraining the defendants from removing outside those of their assets within the jurisdiction. The purpose behind this application was of course to ensure that some funds would remain available, against which execution could be made of the judgment the plaintiffs were almost certain to obtain. The circumstances of the case were such that the money was clearly owing, and there was little question of an arguable defence, so that summary judgment was likely. From a practical point of view, therefore, the plaintiffs wanted to preserve the status quo until the mechanics of enforcement could recover some, if not all, of the judgment debt.

Unfortunately, it had not previously been the practice of the English courts to grant an injunction in circumstances where the order was sought to restrain a defendant from disposing of his own property on the grounds of a likelihood that the plaintiff would recover judgment against him. Consequently, following on this established practice, Donaldson J (as he then was) refused the shipowner's application.

No previous plaintiff had appealed against such a refusal, whether because the sums claimed did not warrant challenging what many practitioners considered too rigid a rule to be changed without statutory intervention, or for other valid reasons, but in this case there was an immediate appeal, which came before the Court of Appeal for judgment on 22 May 1975.[1] No cases were cited in argument, and the hearing was again *ex parte*. After a sufficient, but brief, review of the facts, the appeal was allowed, and an injunction was granted restraining the defendant charterers from disposing of their assets in England outside the jurisdiction on the basis of section 45(1) of the Supreme Court of Judicature (Consolidation) Act 1925, which provided:

> The High Court may grant a mandamus or an injunction or appoint a receiver, by an interlocutory order in all cases in which it appears to the court to be just and convenient so to do.

Uppermost as a consideration was the fear that if some restraint were not imposed the funds would be sent overseas and be difficult to recover, if not irrecoverable. Consequently, in the words of Lord Denning MR[2]:

> There is no reason why the High Court or this court should not make an order such as is asked for here ... There is a strong *prima facie* case that the hire is owing and unpaid. If an injunction is not granted, these monies may be removed out of the jurisdiction and the shipowners will have the greatest difficulty in recovering anything.

Geoffrey Lane L J was of the same opinion[3]:

> In the circumstances which exist in this case there is no reason why the court should not assist a litigant who is in danger of losing money to which he is admittedly entitled.

Thus began the practice which is now undoubtedly one of the most useful to a party faced with an opponent who is likely to so arrange his affairs as to frustrate a court judgment or arbitral award against him. Nevertheless, the departure from established practice raises certain questions, not least the reason why it had previously been

---

[1] *Nippon Yusen Kaisha* v. *Karageorgis and another* [1975] 1 WLR 1093, CA. (22 May 1975); Lord Denning MR, Browne and Geoffrey Lane L JJ.
[2] *Ibid*, at p. 1095, A–B.
[3] *Ibid*, at p. 1095, D.

thought that there was no power to make such an interlocutory order,[4] and why it was opportune for the courts to
change their practice in the economic and social climate of
the 1970s.[5]

A month later, almost before full realization of the Court
of Appeal judgment had alerted commercial practitioners
generally to the chances of success on any future application
for a similar injunction, the question was again considered
by the Court of Appeal, in the case which gave its name to
this particular type of order.[6]

The facts were similar to the earlier *Nippon Yusen Kaisha*
case, and involved shipowners and charterers. The shipowners had let the vessel *Mareva* on a time charterparty for
a trip to the Far East. The charterers had subchartered her
on a voyage charterparty to the President of India, and by
the terms of that subcharter 90 per cent of the freight was
payable against documents issued by the ship, with the
remaining 10 per cent payable later. The vessel loaded fertilizer at Bordeaux on 29 May 1975 for carriage to India, and
the Indian High Commission paid the freight then due
(£174,000) to the charterers in London. The shipowners were
paid two instalments of the half-monthly hire, but were not
paid the third instalment due on 12 June 1975. Further, the
charterers said that they were unable to pay, despite having
the funds from the Indian government, and were about to
cease trading. The shipowners therefore issued a writ on 20
June, claiming the unpaid hire (US $30,800) and damages
for repudiation.

Here, too, the shipowners feared that the charterers
would dispose of their funds before execution of the judgment likely to be given against them, and an application
was made *ex parte* for an injunction restraining the defendants. This was heard by Donaldson J, as he then was, to
whom the Japanese shipowners in *Nippon Yusen Kaisha*
had applied. On consideration of *Lister & Co* v. *Stubbs*[7] the

[4] Discussed in Chapter 2.
[5] Discussed later, p. 11, and in Chapter 2.
[6] *Mareva Compania Naviera SA* v. *International Bulkcarriers SA* [1975] 2 Lloyd's Rep. 509, CA. (23 June 1975); Lord Denning MR, Roskill and Ormrod L JJ.
[7] (1890) 45 Ch D 1, CA, not argued or considered in the *Nippon Yusen Kaisha* case.

injunction was granted only until 17.00 hours on 23 June
1975, out of deference to the Court of Appeal decision in the
previous case, so that the court could be able to consider
itself the view of Donaldson J that he had no jurisdiction to
grant the order.

The appeal was also *ex parte*. Lord Denning MR stated
his view as clearly as before (despite the reservations of the
court in *Lister & Co* v. *Stubbs*[7]) again based on section 45 of
the Supreme Court of Judicature (Consolidation) Act 1925[8]:

> If it appears that the debt is due and owing—and there is a
> danger that the debtor may dispose of his assets so as to defeat
> it before judgment—the court has jurisdiction in a proper case
> to grant an interlocutory judgment so as to prevent him dispo-
> sing of those assets.

Roskill LJ put his views equally strongly[9]:

> On the evidence the defendant time charterers have already
> received £174,000 from the voyage charterers. Yet they have
> sent a telex to the plaintiff shipowners in London on June 17
> stating that their efforts to raise further financial support have
> been fruitless and that they have no alternative but to stop
> trading. If therefore this court does not interfere by injunction,
> it is apparent that the plaintiffs will suffer a grave injustice
> which this court has power to help avoid—the injustice being
> that the ship will have to continue on her voyage to India and
> perhaps—as is not unknown in Indian ports—wait a long time
> there for discharge without remuneration while the defendant
> will be able to dissipate that £174,000.

Thus the course of the *Mareva* injunction was corrected to
accord with the cases referred to by the Court of Appeal,[10]
and although no *inter partes* hearing had yet explored the
wide range of possible arguments, the opportunity to insti-
tute a radical change in the law, provided for initially by

[8] [1975] 2 Lloyd's Rep. 509, at p. 510.
[9] *Ibid*, at p. 511.
[10] *Beddow* v. *Beddow* (1878) 9 Ch D 89, CA; *North London Railway Co* v.
Great Northern Railway Co (1883) 11 QBD 30 CA; *Lister & Co* v. *Stubbs*
(1890) 45 Ch D 1, CA; *Nippon Yusen Kaisha* v. *Karageorgis* [1975] 2 Lloyd's
Rep. 137, CA; see discussion in Chapter 2.

the *Nippon Yusen Kaisha* case,[11] was well set to provide plaintiffs in a wide range of actions[12] with a means to prevent actual and intended defendants making themselves judgment-proof.

It must be noted, though, that the *Mareva* was still an exceptional remedy, based on discretion. In the first *inter partes* hearing in the Court of Appeal, in *MBPXL Corporation* v. *Intercontinental Banking Corporation*,[13] where there was a claim for US $597,000, with interest, against an Anguillan-registered corporation, an appeal against the refusal of Milmo J to restrain the defendants was dismissed, because the plaintiffs had not shown that the defendants had any assets within the jurisdiction. Stephenson L J emphasized that the *Mareva* was an exceptional remedy, and Scarman L J (as he then was) pointed out that[14]: "It is an injunction which can have the most inhibitory and restraining effect upon defendants, and therefore should only be issued if justice and convenience require it."

The next stage in the development of the *Mareva* was the Court of Appeal judgment in *Rasu Maritima SA* v. *Perusahaan Pertambangan Minyah Dan Gas Bumi Negara*.[15] This case, as with *MBPXL* above, was argued *inter partes*, and arose out of the expansion of the Indonesian economy in the 1960s, and the placement of huge orders overseas for ships and other capital equipment. The claim was by a Liberian company, against an Indonesian State-owned corporation,

[11] ". . . a case came before us which started off the greatest piece of judicial law reform in my time"—Denning, *The Due Process of Law* (1980), at p. 134.

[12] The present and future scope of *Marevas* is considered later, in Chapters 4, 7, 10 and 11; for examples of early decisions in non-shipping matters see *Chartered Bank* v. *Daklouche and another* [1980] 1 WLR 107, CA (16 March 1979)—repayment of overdraft; *Allen and others* v. *Jambo Holdings Ltd and others* [1980] 1 WLR 1252, CA (20 July 1979)—claim under the Fatal Accidents Act 1976; *Dellborg* v. *Corix*, 1980 CAT 541 (26 June 1980)—claim against freeholders of luxury flats in St James's Square by the occupants; *Kirby* v. *Banks*, 1980 CAT 624 (1 July 1980)—claim for damages for fraud.

[13] 1975 CAT 411 (28 August 1975), Stephenson and Scarman L JJ.

[14] 1975 CAT 411/5 E–F; it is perhaps surprising that this case was not reported—on the other hand the *Mareva* case itself was only to be found in *Lloyd's Law Reports* until several years after judgment.

[15] Sometimes cited as *Pertamina*; [1978] 1 QB 644, CA (9 March 1977), Lord Denning MR, Orr L J.

for damages of almost £2 million for breach of a charterparty concerning an oil tanker. The writ was issued on 11 August 1976, and on 7 February 1977 Kerr J, as he then was, granted an interim injunction restraining the defendants (Pertamina) from removing certain assets from the Liverpool docks. On 23 February 1977 the interim injunction was discharged, with a stay pending appeal. On 2 March 1977 the appeal hearing began, and a full and comprehensive review of the law took place.

One of the reasons for the discharge of the injunction by Kerr J was that the plaintiffs' case did not at that stage look strong enough for Order 14 summary judgment.[16] Lord Denning MR stated that the plaintiffs had to show a good arguable case,[17] not that success under Order 14 was certain or likely, and this was a most helpful guideline for future applicants. Further, Kerr J had doubted whether the assets, which were part of a fertilizer plant unconnected with the hire of the oil tanker at the centre of the dispute, could be the subject-matter of restraint, but it was held that the discretionary remedy under section 45[18] applied to the defendant's assets generally in the jurisdiction, subject to the test of whether such a restraint was just and convenient.[19] In the circumstances, because the fertilizer plant was worth almost US $12 million to the defendants, but only had a scrap value (its value to the plaintiffs) of approximately US $350,000, and because there was a question as to the true ownership of the equipment, an injunction was refused.

Thus far the *Mareva* was still in an early stage of development. Its use was increasing, and its application to matters outside shipping and commercial circles was beginning, so that interest in the principles on which it was based was widespread outside the comparatively close commercial world where it had first been welcomed. In one respect, however, the *Mareva*'s development was hampered by the fact that applications, except in the Chancery Division, were

[16] The plaintiffs' case in both *Nippon* and *Mareva* essentially satisfied this test.
[17] [1978] 1 QB 644, p. 661.
[18] Supreme Court of Judicature (Consolidation) Act 1925.
[19] [1978] 1 QB 644, at pp. 660, 662, 664.

in chambers, and few defendants challenged the order by applying for a variation or discharge on an *inter partes* hearing. Still fewer took cases to appeal, and there was thus little scope for operational and legal guidelines to be set out in open court, whether at first instance or on appeal. Consequently, the Court of Appeal judgment in *Third Chandris Shipping Corporation* v. *Unimarine SA*[20] was the first case in which were stated the general principles for grant of a *Mareva* injunction, and how those should operate in practice. In essence five points were suggested[21]:

(1) The plaintiff should make full and frank disclosure of all matters in his knowledge which are material for the judge to know.

(2) The plaintiff should give particulars of his claim against the defendant, stating the ground of his claim and the amount, and fairly stating the points made against it by the defendant.

(3) The plaintiff should give some grounds for believing that the defendant has assets here.

(4) The plaintiff should give some grounds for believing that there is a risk of the assets being removed before the judgment or award is satisfied.

(5) The plaintiff must give an undertaking in damages—in case he fails in his claim or the injunction turns out to be unjustified.

Applying the guidelines to the present case the injunctions were upheld. The order taken as typical of the *Mareva* from this case is illustrative of the usual wording:

It is ordered and directed that the defendants by their officers, agents or servants or otherwise be restrained and an injunction is hereby granted restraining them from removing from the jurisdiction or otherwise disposing of any of their assets, including and in particular any moneys forming an account

[20] [1979] 1 QB 645, CA (24 May 1979), Lord Denning MR, Lawton and Cumming-Bruce L JJ.

[21] *Per* Lord Denning MR at p. 668. At p. 669 it was said: "In setting out these guidelines, I hope we shall do nothing to reduce the efficacy of the present practice. In it speed is of the essence. *Ex parte* is of the essence. If there is delay, or if adverse warning is given, the assets may well be removed before the injunction can bite."

in the name of the defendants standing at the Bank of Credit
and Commerce International SA, 100, Leadenhall St., London
EC3, save in so far as the sum exceeds US $91,087.25.

It follows from the above guidelines that there is a heavy
responsibility on the part of a party's legal advisers to prepare the evidence that will best testify to the claims made,
whether on the application for an injunction or on a later
application to discharge or vary.[22] It is usual to present this
evidence by affidavit, and sufficient exhibits to the affidavit
to underline a particular point, especially in relation to
credit-worthiness or the usual course of dealings, are vital.[23]
Another change welcomed by most practitioners was the
"assumption" of jurisdiction over defendants based in
England. There had been no distinction expressly drawn
between foreign and English-based defendants in either
Nippon Yusen Kaisha[24] or in *Mareva*,[25] but in *Pertamina* it
was clear that the court had in mind the remedy as applicable only to foreign-based defendants.[26] This view must
have arisen as a result of the facts of the earlier cases, and
because of the need to integrate the cases based on *Lister &
Co* v. *Stubbs*[27] with the 1975 decisions of the Court of
Appeal. The fears of the plaintiffs in the first successful
Mareva application were that the defendant would remove
funds from the jurisdiction, but a fear that no funds would
be available was equally justified if there was evidence to
suggest the dissipation of funds within the jurisdiction. Either
way, the result of dissipation was the same wherever it took
place. Thus, Lord Hailsham reflected a growing unease with
the distinction when he said[28]:

> I believe the truth to be that sooner or later the courts or
> the legislature will have to choose between two alternatives.
> Either the position of a plaintiff making a claim against an
> English-based defendant will have to be altered or the prin-
> ciples of the *Mareva* cases will have to be modified. In any

[22] This point is dealt with more fully in Chapters 4 and 5.
[23] Explained by Lord Denning MR in *Third Chandris* at p. 670, and by
Lawton L J at p. 672.
[24] [1975] 1 WLR 1093, CA.
[25] [1975] 2 Lloyd's Rep. 509, CA.
[26] [1978] 1 QB 644, CA, at pp. 659–661.
[27] (1890) 45 Ch D 1, CA; see Chapter 2.
[28] *The Siskina* [1979] AC 210, HL (26 October 1977), at p. 261.

new def's whereas domiciled may be caught by a mareva.

event it is clear that *Mareva* injunctions cannot be allowed to flourish independently in the Arcadia of the commercial list without being applied in the High Court generally in all cases where plaintiffs and defendants are comparably placed.

It was therefore not surprising that the Court of Appeal, in *Chartered Bank* v. *Daklouche and another* [29] began a gradual change in the judicial attitude towards foreign-based defendants. Lord Denning MR qualified his earlier remarks in *Pertamina* by stating that they only applied to cases where defendants were permanently settled here and had their assets here. This extension was confirmed by Eveleigh L J, who said that the service of proceedings on a defendant within the jurisdiction (in contrast to service under Order 11) could not prevent the imposition of a *Mareva* order.[30]

In April 1980 Sir Robert Megarry V-C[31] held that there was ample jurisdiction to grant a *Mareva* against an English-based defendant because the real factor to consider was the risk of removal of funds. The question of a distinction was put in robust terms[32]:

Is it really to be said that in relation to *Mareva* injunctions, there is one law for the foreigner and another for the English, and that this flows from a statutory power to grant an injunction if it appears to the court to be "just or convenient" to do so? I cannot see any sensible ground for holding that in this respect there is some privilege or immunity for the English and Welsh.

In *Rahman (Prince Abdul) bin Turki al Sudairy* v. *Abu-Taha and another* [33] the Court of Appeal firmly established that a *Mareva* injunction could be granted against a defendant even if based in England, so long as the circumstances

[29] [1980] 1 WLR 107, CA (16 March 1979), Lord Denning MR, Eveleigh L J, Sir Stanley Rees.

[30] Lord Denning MR at pp. 112–13, Eveleigh L J at p. 115.

[31] [1980] 1 WLR 1259 (Ch D) (21 April 1980).

[32] At p. 1264.

[33] [1980] 1 WLR 1268, CA (June 1980), Lord Denning MR, Waller and Dunn L JJ; in *Bank Leumi (UK) Ltd* v. *Ricky George Sportain (UK) Ltd* 1979 CAT 753 (1 November 1979) Brightman L J (as he then was) had said: "I am not certain in my own mind, in the absence of full argument and consideration, that there is no jurisdiction to grant a *Mareva* injunction against a defendant company within the jurisdiction."

were such that the risk existed of a dissipation of assets, which meant that the plaintiff would not get an eventual judgment satisfied. This was an *inter partes* hearing, and just over two weeks later, in *Kirby* v. *Banks*[34], a *Mareva* against an English-based defendant was ordered on an *ex parte* hearing. The distinction between defendants on the basis of residence was gone. To consolidate this practice, the enactment of the new Supreme Court Act in 1981 was used to add a further subsection to the provisions of section 45 of the 1925 Act, and to alter the wording with the addition of the words "or final" in subsection (1), so that the statutory basis of the *Mareva*, in section 37 of the Supreme Court Act 1981, reads as follows:

(1) The High Court may by order (whether interlocutory or final) grant an injunction or appoint a receiver in all cases in which it appears to the court to be just and convenient to do so.

(2) Any such order may be made either unconditionally or on such terms and conditions as the court thinks just.

(3) The power of the High Court under subsection (1) to grant an interlocutory injunction restraining a party to any proceedings from removing from the jurisdiction of the High Court, or otherwise dealing with, assets located within that jurisdiction shall be exercisable in cases where that party is, as well as in cases where he is not, domiciled resident or present within that jurisdiction.[35]

---

[34] 1980 CAT 624 (1 July 1980).

[35] Subsections (4) and (5) read: (4) The power of the High Court to appoint a receiver by way of equitable execution shall operate in relation to all legal estates and interests in land; and that power—(a) may be exercised in relation to an estate or interest in land whether or not a charge has been imposed on that land under section 1 of the Charging Orders Act 1979 for the purpose of enforcing the judgment, order or award in question; and (b) shall be in addition to, and not in derogation of, any power of any court to appoint a receiver in proceedings for enforcing such a charge. (5) Where an order under the said section 1 imposing a charge for the purpose of enforcing a judgment, order or award has been, or has effect as if, registered under section 6 of the Land Charges Act 1972, subsection (4) of the said section 6 (effect of non-registration of writs and orders registrable under that section) shall not apply to an order appointing a receiver made either—(a) in proceedings for enforcing the charge; or (b) by way of equitable execution of the judgment, order or award or, as the case may be, of so much of it as requires payment of moneys secured by the charge.

The need for the "Mareva"

The single most effective reason for granting a *Mareva* injunction is, in practical terms, encompassed within the need to prevent a defendant snapping his fingers[36] at a judgment of the court with financial impunity, because he has arranged his affairs so as to leave no worthwhile assets within the reach of the plaintiff judgment creditor.

To allow a defendant to escape his obligations in such a way would be to weaken the effectiveness of the English civil legal system, and some protection of litigants is therefore necessary. As will be discussed later,[37] the applicant for a *Mareva*, whether plaintiff or counterclaiming defendant, has to show a good arguable case that he will succeed at the trial, and that the refusal of an injunction would involve a real risk that an eventual judgment or arbitral award in his favour would remain unsatisfied.[38] Further, the position of persons other than the litigants is protected by the need to avoid disruption to the interests of third parties, and the principle that injunctions which affect third parties must be drafted as clearly as possible.[39] Therefore it may be said that a judge, when hearing an application for a *Mareva* injunction, balances the position of the respective parties, in so far as is explained or clear to him, and uses his own discretion and experience to decide the merits of the application. For this reason the Court of Appeal is reluctant to interfere with the exercise of that discretion.[40]

As a result, the imposition of a *Mareva* is not something lightly ordered. It may be asked why it has been necessary

[36] See Lord Denning MR in *Pertamina* [1978] 1 QB 644, at p. 661, referring to the words of Kerr J.
[37] See generally Chapters 3, 4 and 5.
[38] *Ninemia Maritime Corporation* v. *Trave Schiffahrtsgesellschaft mbH und Co KG (The Niedersachsen)* [1983] 1 WLR 1412, CA (29 July 1983), Eveleigh, Kerr and Dillon L JJ.
[39] See, *inter alia*, *Z Ltd* v. *A-Z and AA-LL* [1982] 1 QB 558, CA (16 December 1981), Lord Denning MR, Eveleigh and Kerr L JJ; *Iraqi Ministry of Defence* v. *Arcepey Shipping Co SA (The Angel Bell)* [1980] 1 Lloyd's Rep. 632, QBD Commercial Ct., Goff J; *Cretanor Maritime Co Ltd* v. *Irish Marine Management Ltd* [1978] 1 WLR 966, CA (15 February 1978), Buckley and Goff L JJ, Sir David Cairns; *Searose Ltd* v. *Seatrain (UK) Ltd* [1981] 1 WLR 894, Goff J; see also later, Chapter 6.
[40] See *Ninemia* [1983] 1 WLR 1412, CA.

to develop this discretionary jurisdiction at all, especially as the remedy is barely a decade old?

The answer must be in the rapid change in commercial and banking practice since the Second World War, and the increasing anonymity of international businesses and traders. It is no longer possible to rely on personal knowledge of the parties to transactions, still less to vouch for them to others, and the great competition there is in the shipping and international trade world, together with the profits to be made in carefully constructed deals, present many opportunities for contracts to be broken or debts unpaid. The recovery of damages or debts is made more difficult by the ease with which an unscrupulous litigant can remove his funds from country to country, often in complete secrecy.

There is, of course, a distinction between outright fraud (such as the International Maritime Bureau in London has been set up to counter) with its mixture of insurance fraud, counterfeiting, trade-mark infringement, and piracy, and the litigant whose dishonesty arises at the time when his debts are due. Nevertheless, the *Mareva* is equally useful in the right circumstances against all types of non-payer, and the number of judgment debtors who try to evade their debts is increasing, for a simple reason. An outstanding judgment has, of itself, little effect on a party likely to evade his obligations. The important fact for him, made easier by the cloak of incorporation, is the non-payment of his liabilities. Left to his own devices, and astute to the possibility of obstructing the course of litigation in any event, he would willingly accept any stigma associated with an outstanding judgment. In fact, a putative plaintiff may not proceed to action against a defendant without some assets within available reach, because of the costs and inconvenience involved in obtaining an empty judgment. Armed with a *Mareva* injunction, on the other hand, the plaintiff can pray in aid the considerable power of the court to restrain the defendant pending resolution of a dispute, and this can, it is submitted, only assist the administration of justice to the great benefit of all concerned.

Speed is required in applying for a *Mareva* to maintain the element of surprise. An *ex parte* application is therefore vital, as it is hardly consistent with the fear of a defendant dissipating his assets if not restrained, to give him advance notice of the hearing. If granted, however, subsequent applications should be *inter partes* if at all possible. In fact, an application to discharge a *Mareva* is comparatively rare, which may point to a justification of the order, or may indicate its success in forcing a defendant to settle.[41] Either way, the *Mareva* is now a valuable service to the litigant, still utilized for the most part in the Commercial Court, but common in other divisions of the High Court, and used in appropriate cases in the County Court.

In Chapter 4 the procedure in applying for a *Mareva* is examined, but before that we must consider further the background to the present procedure in Chapters 2 and 3.

[41] These points are discussed more fully in Chapters 4 and 5.

CHAPTER 2

The background to the "Mareva" before 1975

Before 1975 an interlocutory injunction against the disposal of assets by a defendant, as we have considered in Chapter 1, was contrary to established practice. The judicial attitude was that there was no inherent power to grant such an order, and no statutory provision or rule of court that could be used to support a change. The *Nippon Yusen Kaisha*[1] case removed doubts about the possibility of an injunction, but without either full argument or considering the effect of earlier cases, said to show the lack of jurisdiction, or its general undesirability. In *Mareva*[2] the earlier cases were considered. It is necessary therefore to look at these as they still form a base from which the *Mareva* injunction may be criticized or restricted by those who hold the opinion that it is a remedy to be confined to special circumstances.

In *Robinson* v. *Pickering*[3] the plaintiff was a tradesman, and the defendants were husband and wife. The wife had been supplied with goods on credit, and owed the plaintiff over £436. He sought a charge on her separate estate, for which the husband and wife were both trustees, and in the meantime an injunction to restrain her and her husband from dealing with the assets. Malins V-C granted an injunction, but on appeal the Court of Appeal held that no injunction could be permitted. The clear statement of James L J, that: "You cannot get an injunction to restrain a man who is alleged to be a debtor from parting with his property" was in fact an observation, albeit a weighty one, to counsel for the plaintiff.[4] It was not in the judgments, although these were clear in their rejection of the order sought. However,

[1] [1975] 1 WLR 1093, CA.
[2] [1975] 2 Lloyd's Rep. 509, CA.
[3] (1881) 16 Ch D 660, CA.
[4] *Ibid*, at p. 661, James L J to Dundas Gardiner.

much of the argument appears to have centred on the difficulty of enforcing a debt against a married woman, but James L J held that: ". . . a creditor is no more entitled to such an injunction as this against a married woman than he would be entitled to it against a man."[5]

Prima facie, this case is good authority against the grant of an injunction, except that little is known of the potential risk involved in not granting one; it is clear that the plaintiff did have a very strong case. Lord Denning MR distinguished the decision on the grounds that no foreign defendant was involved[6] although it was seen in Chapter 1 that the requirement of a foreign defendant soon evaporated after 1975 because of the need to keep the *Mareva* flexible and impartial as to a defendant's residence or place of business.[7]

In *Lister & Co* v. *Stubbs*[8] the facts were that the plaintiffs were silk-spinners and dyers, who employed the defendant as their foreman of works. He had an additional responsibility to buy factory material, and was allegedly paid by a supplier company on a commission basis for goods he had ordered on the plaintiffs' behalf. It was claimed that he had made over £5,500 in this way, and the plaintiffs started an action against him for the sums received corruptly, as well as damages, an account, and an inquiry. They also asked for an interlocutory injunction to prevent him dealing with land which he had bought with the money, and for an order that his investments and spare money be paid into court. Stirling J refused the injunction, and on appeal much of the argument was again unconnected with the injunction, but centred on the alleged trust nature of the defendant's possession of the money and the land. A further diversion is that the money had of course been paid directly by the supplier company to the defendant, and was arguably never the plaintiffs' money.

The decision was broadly based on the plaintiffs' lack of legal basis for their proprietary claim. In addition, the

[5] *Ibid*, at p. 663.
[6] In *Pertamina* [1978] 1 QB 644, CA, at p. 659 F–G; the same distinction was made regarding the cases discussed below.
[7] See above p. 11.
[8] (1890) 45 Ch D 1, CA.

consequence of an order to pay into court was considered unacceptable because it would give a plaintiff priority against other creditors.[9] Cotton L J stated[10]:

> ... if the money sought to be recovered is not the money of the plaintiffs, we should be simply ordering the defendant to pay into Court a sum of money in his possession because there is a *prima facie* case against him that at the hearing it will be established that he owes money to the plaintiffs. In my opinion, that would be wrong in principle ... if we were to order the defendant to give the security asked for, it would be introducing an entirely new and wrong principle—which we ought not to do, even though we might think that, having regard to the circumstances of the case, it would be highly just to make the order.

There was no argument as to risk of dissipation, and it is submitted that this case is not strong authority for a lack of jurisdiction in the High Court to grant *Mareva*-type injunctions. It should also be noted that leave to defend an action is frequently made conditional on payment of money into court, even though the case is by no means certain for the plaintiff, and this is precisely the type of security objected to.

Later cases concerned matrimonial property, such as *Newton* v. *Newton*,[11] *Burmester* v. *Burmester*,[12] *Jagger* v. *Jagger*,[13] and *Scott* v. *Scott*,[14] but these may not only be distinguished on their facts, but also disregarded as adverse authority because of the statutory power the Family Division now has to restrain a respondent in circumstances directly similar to those cases. This notable exception to the practice against granting injunctions to restrain one party to litigation from disposing of his assets was, many years

[9] See Lindley L J at p. 15.
[10] At p. 14.
[11] (1885) 11 PD 11—Sir James Hannen P, at p. 13: "It is not competent for a court, merely *quia timet*, to restrain a defendant from dealing with his property"; the respondent may in fact have been based abroad.
[12] [1913] P 76.
[13] [1926] P 93—Scrutton L J at p. 102: "I am not aware of any statutory or other power in the court to restrain a person from dealing with his property at a time when no order against him has been made."
[14] [1951] P 193.

before the first *Mareva* cases, provided for by the Matrimonial Causes Act, now section 37(2)(*a*) of the Matrimonial Causes Act 1973, which provides:

> (2) Where proceedings for financial relief are brought by one person against another, the court may, on the application of the first-mentioned person—
>
> > (*a*) if it is satisfied that the other party to the proceedings is, with the intention of defeating the claim for financial relief, about to make any disposition or to transfer out of the jurisdiction or otherwise deal with any property, make such order as it thinks fit for restraining the other party from so doing or otherwise for protecting the claim;

The proceedings for financial relief mentioned will essentially include any money claim against the other party before remarriage of the applicant, and under subsection (6), disposition includes any conveyance, assurance or gift of property of any description, except those resulting from a will or codicil. Thus the proceeds of sale of the family home, and its contents, as well as savings, are all included in the property which can be frozen. This power is regularly exercised in the Family Division, and is especially protective when the applicant is married to someone domiciled abroad, or with family or business connections overseas. There is no requirement to show an overseas element, however, and the threat of disposal of property within England is equally significant. The test of risk is weaker than in the *Mareva* jurisdiction, in practical terms, because the very nature and cause of the marital proceedings can provide substantial evidence of the likelihood of a disposition or transfer, but there is no general power to freeze a respondent's property merely because he is alleged to be the type of person who would try to defeat the wife's claim.[15]

The power is given added strength by section 37(2)(*b*), which provides that the court may:

> (*b*) if it is satisfied that the other party has, with that intention, made a reviewable disposition and that if the dispo-

---

[15] *Smith* v. *Smith* (1973) 117 SJ 525; see also *Quartermain* v. *Quartermain* (1974) 118 SJ 597; *Jackson* v. *Jackson* (1978) 9 Fam Law 56, CA; *Roche* v. *Roche* (1981) 11 Fam Law 243, CA; and see later Chapter 4.

sition were set aside financial relief or different financial relief would be granted to the applicant, make an order setting aside the disposition;

Thus, at a time when interim injunctions in other cases where property was at risk of being disposed of were regularly refused, the Family Division could not only freeze a respondent's assets, but also order the avoidance of transactions designed to frustrate the assessment and enforcement of a claim. This power was seemingly accepted as consistent with the court's duty to judge such proceedings fairly and equitably, and no criticism seems to have been sustained that many applicants were (and are) legally aided, and not immediately good for any undertaking in damages, if this were given.[16] Further, the power to freeze assets is exercisable by a Registrar after the main proceedings have been started,[17] whereas an injunction generally is an order for a judge to grant, except in limited cases in the Queen's Bench Division, such as where the order is by consent.[18] Certainly, a *Mareva* injunction, which has a close similarity to the Family Division injunction, is not an order a Master can grant, and if there is a possibility of consent to a *Mareva*-type order, it is submitted that the proper practice is for an undertaking to be given by the party concerned, rather than a request to the Master to initial a consent *Mareva* order.

It thus remains to decide whether the assumption of the *Mareva* power in 1975 was consistent with the approach of the courts in any other field.[19] As a starting point, the Admiralty jurisdiction of the High Court can be considered.

[16] But see also *Allen and others* v. *Jambo Holdings and others* [1980] 1 WLR 1251, CA at p. 1257 A–B, and later p. 36.

[17] Matrimonial Causes Rules 1977, rule 84. The Registrar probably also has power to grant an injunction by consent in proceedings under the Married Women's Property Act 1882.

[18] See Order 32, rule 11(2); also Order 50, rule 9—injunction ancillary to charging order; order 51, rule 2—injunction ancillary to appointment of receiver by way of equitable execution.

[19] The court can only grant an injunction when there is a legal or equitable right, *The Siskina* [1979] AC 210, HL; this point is discussed in Chapter 3. The *Mareva* jurisdiction was not challenged in *The Siskina*, and impliedly approved, see Lord Diplock at p. 254, and Lord Hailsham at p. 261.

The Admiralty Court has always exercised an *in rem* jurisdiction over ships within the English jurisdiction. This power is now contained in the Supreme Court Act 1981,[20] and covers a wide range of claims, under section 20(2), including the ownership of ships, loss of or damage to goods carried in a ship, claims for towage and salvage, and claims by a master or crew member for wages. This *in rem* jurisdiction also applies to aircraft.[21]

The practice of the Admiralty Court is not something viewed generally as excessive or unwarranted, although Admiralty law does have a pedigree most legal principles, even those based on commercial law and the old *lex mercatoria*, do not have. However, the *in rem* procedure is not only sanctioned in objective terms by long and satisfactory use, but also by consistent application, albeit with some differences, by all seafaring nations. The accession of major maritime countries to the 1952 Brussels Convention on the Arrest of Sea-Going Ships is witness to the international acceptance of the Admiralty jurisdiction.

In England, the arrest of a ship under the Supreme Court Act 1981 perfects the security of a plaintiff's claim, so that a maritime lien exists, which makes the plaintiff a secured creditor, subject only to the claims of other secured creditors.[22] The *Mareva* injunction, although it may have the effect of inducing a defendant to put up security in the same way as the threat of arrest does in admiralty actions, gives no security in the property frozen.[23] Therefore, it is actually less effective in law than the long-established *in rem* action, although its practical pressure on a defendant cannot be denied. In comparison, the *Mareva* is consistent with this traditional legal response to the international nature of commerce, and the need to protect innocent parties. It is a justifiable step to extend this protection to all litigants, and the interim preservative or protective measure is well

[20] Sections 20–22; Order 75; previously under the Administration of Justice Act 1956.
[21] Supreme Court Act 1981, s.20(7).
[22] *The Monica S* [1968] P 741; *Re Aro Co Ltd* [1980] 1 All ER 1067; *The Falcon* [1981] 1 Lloyd's Rep. 13.
[23] See *Cretanor Maritime Co Ltd* v. *Irish Marine Management Ltd* [1978] 1 WLR 966, CA, and see later p. 62.

known in other countries and jurisdictions, both civil law
and common law based, as can be seen in Chapter 11.

Apart from the specific example just given, are there
instances of judicial flexibility, with the similar aim of doing
justice in the circumstances of a case? It is submitted that
the history of English law in the 20th century is full of
examples of judicial development. To take but a few, the
courts have intervened in "family" cases, even though this
was a departure from previous practice.[24] They have also
intervened where there has been a perceived inequality of
bargaining power or duress,[25] and the doctrine of fundamental breach has developed to counter extreme cases of
exclusion clauses.[26] Further, the law protects creditors where
there has been attempted avoidance of the obligations of a
debtor towards his creditors by the transfer of property,[27]
and the subject of execution of judgments against debtors
who had made themselves proof against execution was seen
as sufficiently serious in the 1960s to prompt the Payne Committee Report,[28] which recommended much stronger con-
trols on the evasion of judgment debts.

The concept of blocking a person's property is not alien to
England. On the administrative side, the government had
until 1979 wide powers to prevent assets in the United Kingdom from being removed abroad, and these were exercised

[24] See as examples *Pettit* v. *Pettit* [1970] AC 777, HL; *Gissing* v. *Gissing*
[1971] AC 886, HL; *Heseltine* v. *Heseltine* [1971] 1 All ER 952, CA; *Eves* v.
Eves [1975] 3 All ER 768; *CA*; *Burns* v. *Burns* [1984] Ch 317, CA. Also
consider the earlier cases of *Rimmer* v. *Rimmer* [1953] 1 QB 67, and *Fribance* v. *Fribance* [1957] 1 WLR 384.

[25] *Lloyds Bank Ltd.* v. *Bundy* [1975] QB 326; see *Clifford Davis Management Ltd* v. *WEA Records Ltd* [1975] 1 WLR 61; *North Ocean Shipping Co
Ltd* v. *Hyundai Construction Co Ltd* [1979] QB 705.

[26] But see *Photo Production Ltd* v. *Securicor Transport Ltd* [1980] AC
827, HL, overruling the Court of Appeal. Also *Suisse Atlantique Soc. d'
Armement Maritime SA* v. *NV Rotterdamsche Kolen Centrale* [1967] 1
AC 361, HL.

[27] See the Law of Property Act 1925, s.172; the Bankruptcy Act 1914, s.44;
the Companies Act 1948, s. 320; *Peat* v. *Gresham Trust Ltd* [1934] AC 252,
HL; *Re Eric Holmes (Property) Ltd* [1965] Ch 1052; *Re Ramsey* [1913] 2 KB
80.

[28] Chaired by Mr Justice Payne, Report of the Committee on the Enforcement of Judgment Debts, 1969 (HMSO, Cmnd 3909); see especially paras.
1245 to 1260. The opportunity was not taken to suggest a *Mareva*-type
order under the then applicable provision of s.45 of the Supreme Court of
Judicature (Consolidation) Act 1925.

for reasons of economic policy against all persons, regardless of obligation.[29]

In the light of the above, of necessity a short comparison, the development of the *Mareva* injunction is not a fundamental deviation from established principles of English law, but instead reflects a growing flexibility in the attitude of the courts to assisting litigants. It is judicial law-making because of the need for discretion and an objective view of new situations as and when they arise. No statutory enactment which sought to cover exclusively the potential use of a *Mareva* could succeed because of the nature of the remedy applied for, in varied and changing circumstances. Consequently, the *Mareva* represents the combination of judicial and statutory power to answer the activities of defendants who try to evade, deliberately, judgment and arbitral awards. It is part of the need to ensure that justice is done.[30]

It may also be said that the broad views of the judges in the earlier cases are valid. There is no general right to attach the goods of a party simply because he is an actual or alleged debtor. There must be a risk of dissipation, and the *Mareva* order as the maintenance of the status quo does not give the plaintiff any legal or equitable right in the property which he does not already enjoy. The *Mareva* is still an exception to what can be called the *Lister & Co* v. *Stubbs* principle, and in granting the order the court has to take a risk but, as Sir Robert Megarry V-C observed in *Barclay-Johnson* v. *Yuill*,[31] it is better to err on the side of conservation rather than dispersion.

---

[29] Exchange Control Act 1947. The powers were withdrawn, but not abolished, in 1979 (see SI 1979 (1660)).
[30] See the observations of Sir John Donaldson MR in *Buckland* v. *Palmer* [1984] 1 WLR 1109, CA, at p. 1115 (not a *Mareva* case); contrast the continued application of categorization (between tort and contract) which resulted in an important difference of approach under the Law Reform (Frustrated Contracts) Act 1943, in *Basildon District Council* v. *J E Lesser (Properties) Ltd* [1984] 3 WLR 812.
[31] [1980] 1 WLR 1259, at p. 1266, H.

CHAPTER 3

The background to the "Mareva" after 1975

After 1975 the number of cases involving *Marevas* has increased to such an extent that each working day sees applications in the High Court, and in appropriate cases outside court hours directly to a judge. The scope for leading cases is therefore wide, and significant decisions have included *Pertamina*,[1] *The Siskina*,[2] *Cretanor Maritime Co Ltd* v. *Irish Marine Management Ltd*[3]—the question of a secured interest, *Third Chandris Shipping Corporation* v. *Unimarine SA*[4]—Court of Appeal guidelines, *Allen and others* v. *Jambo Holdings Ltd and others*[5]—order against an aircraft, *Barclay-Johnson* v. *Yuill*[6]—order against an English-based defendant, *Banker's Trust Co* v. *Shapira and others*[7]—tracing of assets, *AJ Bekhor & Co Ltd* v. *Bilton*[8]—discovery, *Z Ltd* v. *A-Z & AA-LL*[9]—position of banks and third parties, and *Ninemia*[10]—new guidelines.

These are all relevant in various aspects of the *Mareva* jurisdiction, but this chapter seeks to outline arguably the most important to arise, that of the inherent jurisdiction of the court to grant an injunction only in support of a legal or equitable right, within the jurisdiction of the English

[1] [1978] 1 QB 644, CA (9 March 1977), Lord Denning MR and Orr L J.
[2] [1979] AC 210, HL (26 October 1977).
[3] [1978] 1 WLR 966, CA (15 February 1978), Buckley and Goff L JJ, Sir David Cairns.
[4] [1979] 1 QB 645, CA (24 May 1979), Lord Denning MR, Lawton and Cumming-Bruce L JJ.
[5] [1980] 1 WLR 1251, CA (20 July 1979), Lord Denning MR, Shaw and Templeman L JJ.
[6] [1980] 1 WLR 1259, Ch D (21 April 1980), Sir Robert Megarry V-C.
[7] [1980] 1 WLR 1274, CA (4 June 1980), Lord Denning MR, Waller and Dunn L JJ.
[8] [1981] 1 QB 923, CA (6 February 1981), Stephenson, Ackner and Griffiths L JJ.
[9] [1982] 1 QB 558, CA (16 December 1981), Lord Denning MR, Eveleigh and Kerr L JJ.
[10] [1983] 1 WLR 1412, CA (29 July 1983), Eveleigh and Dillon L JJ.

courts. This essential twin test means that a *Mareva* is completely ancillary to a claim, regardless of the fact that in practice it is the *Mareva* order, and not the writ, which often ends the dispute between the parties because of its effect, and because no appearance is entered by the defendant to oppose either the writ or the injunction, and judgment is enforced against the injuncted property to satisfy the judgment debt.

The practical operation of the *Mareva* must not confuse the question of whether there is a legal right, within the jurisdiction of the English courts, that can be assisted by an interlocutory or final injunction.[11]

The first case to consider is *The North London Railway Co* v. *The Great Northern Railway Co*.[12] This confirmed the view that the Judicature Act 1873 dealt with procedure by consolidation, and did not confer any extra substantive rights. The High Court after the Act could still grant an injunction in a case where the issues raised showed a legal or equitable right which existed, or could have existed, before 1873.[13] This leaves open of course the development of legal and equitable rights themselves, so that it is consistent with this case to allow the power of the court to be exercised in support of rights now recognized by the law, whenever they may first have been "discovered". It would be less than logical, as well as highly inconvenient, if the High Court judges today were limited by what was known of the jurisdiction in 1873.[14] In 1883, Cotton L J said[15]:

... is not the *prima facie* presumption that it did not intend to give the right to an injunction to parties who before had no

[11] The question of a *Mareva* in support of a right within the exclusive jurisdiction of a foreign court is discussed in Chapter 10.

[12] (1883) 11 QBD 30, CA.

[13] *Ibid*, per Brett L J at p. 38, and Cotton L J at p. 39.

[14] See especially *Bremer Vulkan Schiffbau und Maschinenfabrik* v. *South India Shipping Corporation* [1981] AC 909, HL; [1980] 1 Lloyd's Rep. 255, CA; [1979] 3 WLR 471, Donaldson J.

[15] (1883) 11 QBD 30 at p. 39. Note that Sir George Jessel MR considered that the section granted unlimited power to grant an injunction where it would be right or just to do so—*Beddow* v. *Beddow* (1878) 9 Ch D 89, CA. Lord Denning MR relied on this view in *Mareva* [1975] 2 Lloyd's Rep. 509, at p. 510; *Beddow* and *North London Railway Co* are reconcilable. The precondition of a legal or equitable right was re-emphasized in *Gouriet* v. *Union of Post Office Workers* [1978] AC 435, HL, see especially Lord Edmund-Davies at p. 516.

legal right whatever, but simply to give to the court, when dealing with legal rights which were under its jurisdiction independently of this section, power, if it should think it just or convenient, to superadd to what would have been previously the remedy, a remedy by way of injunction, altering therefore not in any way the rights of parties so as to give a right to those who had no legal right before, but enabling the court to modify the principle on which it had previously proceeded in granting injunctions, so that where there is a legal right the court may, without being hampered by its old rules, grant an injunction where it is just or convenient to do so for the purpose of protecting or asserting the legal rights of the parties.

These principles leave discretion to the judiciary so long as a right exists. Consequently, as it is the courts which exercise this discretion, it must be the case that the considerations on which *Mareva* orders are based will change as the circumstances of litigation change. It is, as Lord Denning MR has said, all part of the evolutionary process.[16] Assuming therefore that a legal or equitable right exists,[17] the second point to consider is that the English courts must have jurisdiction over the dispute, subject only to the provisions of the 1968 Brussels Convention.[18] Thus, the defendant must be brought within the jurisdiction by being properly summonsed to appear (even if the writ is served on him when he is temporarily present[19]), or by his voluntary submission to the jurisdiction.[20] Apart though

[16] In *Ward* v. *James* [1966] 1 QB 273, CA at p. 295.

[17] Note the discussions in Chapter 7 as to the right of the police to apply for a *Mareva*.

[18] Dealt with in Chapter 10—limited power will exist for the grant of interim relief in England if there is pending litigation in a Convention country.

[19] See generally Order 10; defendants domiciled in a Convention country cannot be served with a writ concerning matters within the scope of the Convention when temporarily present in England, but other parties can, see *Maharanee of Baroda* v. *Wildenstein* [1972] 2 QB 283 (the decision would be different now only as to the particular facts). Note also rules as to partnerships—Order 81, r.1; companies—the Companies Act 1948, ss. 407, 412, 437 and Order 65, r.3; substituted service—Order 65, r.4.

[20] A plaintiff suing in this country submits to the jurisdiction for related counterclaims—*High Commissioner for India* v. *Ghosh* [1960] 1 QB 134; an appearance to contest jurisdiction is not a submission, *Re Dulles' Settlement (No. 2)* [1951] Ch 842.

from the physical presence of a defendant in England, he may also be within the extended or assumed jurisdiction of the courts because of the special rules for issue and service of a writ overseas. These rules are vital in most *Mareva* cases with an international element, and are set out in RSC Order 11. The court has a discretion to give leave for the writ first to be issued and then to be served. These are two distinct procedures, and the first can be granted without the second. To guide an applicant, six main principles have emerged from past cases: first, doubt about granting leave should be in the defendant's favour; second, the plaintiff must make full and fair disclosure of all the facts because the application is *ex parte*; third, care should be taken before any foreigner overseas is summonsed to appear before an English court; fourth, the application must be within the spirit as well as the letter of the rules; fifth, a foreign jurisdiction clause should generally be upheld; and sixth, the court should consider which is the most convenient forum for the dispute.[21] It follows therefore that a plaintiff who successfully obtains leave to issue and serve a writ under Order 11 can also apply for a *Mareva* because jurisdiction will be accepted in the main action.[22] However, the application is *ex parte*; what therefore determines whether the plaintiff has made out a satisfactory case for the assumption of English jurisdiction?

First of all, if there is a choice of jurisdiction clause bringing the matter before the English courts, this is a weighty point, entitled to full consideration. So, too, is an express choice of English law, or circumstances implying such a choice. These will often be the points most relied upon, but in fact Order 11 is very wide. It will not be possible to decide finally on jurisdiction without full argument, and so the applicant has to show that he has a good arguable case on the merits, and that on the same basis the English courts have jurisdiction and should exercise their discretion. The case must therefore be, in all the circumstances, a proper

---

[21] See *The Hagen* [1908] P 189; *Mackender* v. *Feldia* [1967] 1 QB 590; *The Brabo* [1949] AC 326; *Soc Gén de Paris* v. *Dreyfus Bros* (1885) 29 Ch D 239.
[22] The procedure is set out in Chapter 4.

one for service out of the jurisdiction.[23] If the Order 11 jurisdiction is challenged and leave later set aside, the *Mareva* injunction must also be set aside because it has nothing with which it can be linked, unless some new grounds of jurisdiction are available.

In view of the importance of Order 11 it is appropriate to set out the leading provisions[24]:

Principal cases in which service of writ out of jurisdiction is permissible

1.—(1) Provided that the writ does not contain any claim mentioned in Order 75, r.2(1) and is not a writ to which paragraph (2) of this rule applies, service of a writ out of the jurisdiction is permissible with the leave of the Court if in the action begun by the writ—

  (a) relief is sought against a person domiciled within the jurisdiction;

  (b) an injunction is sought ordering the defendant to do or refrain from doing anything within the jurisdiction (whether or not damages are also claimed in respect of a failure to do or the doing of that thing);

  (c) the claim is brought against a person duly served within or out of the jurisdiction and a person out of the jurisdiction is a necessary or proper party thereto;

  (d) the claim is brought to enforce, rescind, dissolve, annul or otherwise affect a contract, or to recover damages or obtain other relief in respect of the breach of a contract, being (in either case) a contract which—

    (i) was made within the jurisdiction, or

    (ii) was made by or through an agent trading or residing within the jurisdiction on behalf of a principal trading or residing out of the jurisdiction, or

    (iii) is by its terms, or by implication, governed by English law, or

    (iv) contains a term to the effect that the High Court shall have jurisdiction to hear and determine any action in respect of the contract;

[23] See cases in fn. 21 above, and *Vitkovice Horni* v. *Korner* [1951] AC 869; *The Siskina* [1979] AC 210, HL.

[24] Order 11, r.1; this rule is the new Order 11, r.1, amended to comply with the Civil Jurisdiction and Judgments Act 1982, and RSC (Amendment No 2) SI 1983 (No 1181). At the time of writing the new order is not yet in force, but implementation is expected as soon as the delays in ratification are ended. Until then, the 1982 edition of the *Supreme Court Practice* ("The White Book"), with current supplement should be referred to.

(e) the claim is brought in respect of a breach committed within the jurisdiction of a contract made within or out of the jurisdiction, and irrespective of the fact, if such be the case, that the breach was preceded or accompanied by a breach committed out of the jurisdiction that rendered impossible the performance of so much of the contract as ought to have been performed within the jurisdiction;

(f) the claim is founded on a tort and the damage was sustained, or resulted from an act committed, within the jurisdiction;

(g) the whole subject-matter of the action is land situate within the jurisdiction (with or without rents or profits) or the perpetuation of testimony relating to land so situate;

(h) the claim is brought to construe, rectify, set aside or enforce an act, deed, will, contract, obligation or liability affecting land situate within the jurisdiction;

(i) the claim is made for a debt secured on immovable property or is made to assert, declare or determine proprietary or possessory rights, or rights of security, in or over movable property, or to obtain authority to dispose of movable property, situate within the jurisdiction;

(j) the claim is brought to execute the trusts of a written instrument being trusts that ought to be executed according to English law and of which the person to be served with the writ is a trustee, or for any relief or remedy which might be obtained in any such action;

(k) the claim is made for the administration of the estate of a person who died domiciled within the jurisdiction or for any relief or remedy which might be obtained in any such action;

(l) the claim is brought in a probate action within the meaning of Order 76;

(m) the claim is brought to enforce any judgment or arbitral award;

(n) the claim is brought against a defendant not domiciled in Scotland or Northern Ireland in respect of a claim by the Commissioners of Inland Revenue for or in relation to any of the duties or taxes which have been, or are for the time being, placed under their care and management;

(o) the claim is brought under the Nuclear Installations

Act 1965 or in respect of contributions under the Social
Security Act 1975;

(*p*) the claim is made for a sum to which the Directive of
the Council of the European Communities dated 15th
March 1976 No. 76/308/EEC applies, and service is to be
effected in a country which is a member State of the
European Economic Community.

(2) Service of a writ out of the jurisdiction is permissible
without the leave of the Court provided that each claim made
by the writ is either:—

(*a*) a claim which by virtue of the Civil Jurisdiction and
Judgments Act 1982 the Court has power to hear and
determine, made in proceedings to which the following
conditions apply—

(i) no proceedings between the parties concerning the
same cause of action are pending in the courts of
any other part of the United Kingdom or of any
other Convention territory, and

(ii) either—
the defendant is domiciled in any part of the United
Kingdom or in any other Convention territory, or
the proceedings begun by the writ are proceedings
to which Article 16 of Schedule 1 or of Schedule 4
refers, or the defendant is a party to an agree-
ment conferring jurisdiction to which Article 17 of
Schedule 1 or of Schedule 4 to that Act applies,

or

(*b*) a claim which by virtue of any other enactment the
High Court has power to hear and determine notwithstanding that the person against whom the claim is
made is not within the jurisdiction of the Court or that
the wrongful act, neglect or default giving rise to the
claim did not take place within its jurisdiction.

It can be seen that these are wide enough to cover most
instances giving rise to a dispute which has some connection
with England. The importance of Order 11 is increased by
the fact that once the writ has been issued and served the
action proceeds in the usual way, so that despite a non-
appearance by the defendant the plaintiff can proceed to
judgment, and this can be enforced against the assets
encompassed within the *Mareva* order. The power of the
court in this assumption of jurisdiction is thus very much a

working part of the *Mareva* jurisdiction generally, and in
practice great care is exercised to ensure that this "exorbitant" jurisdiction is not abused. Of course, some assets must
be in England before a *Mareva* is granted.[25]

The Siskina

The only case yet to include a *Mareva* and be before the
House of Lords is *Siskina (owners of cargo lately laden on
board) and others* v. *Distos Compania Naviera SA (The Siskina)*.[26] In many ways the facts of this case demanded some
form of judicial relief because of the fraud involved.

The defendant shipowners were a one-ship Panamanian
company, who chartered the *Siskina* to Italian charterers
for a voyage to Saudi Arabia. Cargo belonging to a variety
of shippers was loaded, freight prepaid, and bills of lading
were issued, which were transferred to the buyers of the
goods in Saudi Arabia who, having paid in advance for the
cost, insurance and freight involved, were the cargo owners.
The bills of lading contained an exclusive jurisdiction clause
for the Italian courts in Genoa.

After the ship was loaded she set off for Saudi Arabia,
making for the Suez Canal. The charterers, however, had
not paid the charter freight to the shipowners, who therefore refused to take her through the Canal without payment. Although some freight was handed over, the
shipowners refused to go further, and ordered the *Siskina*
to sail to Limassol in Cyprus, where they arrested the cargo
through the Cypriot courts, and asserted a lien against it
for the charter freight. The cargo was unloaded, and the

[25] *Third Chandris Shipping Corp* v. *Unimarine SA* [1979] 1 QB 645, CA
at p. 668, *per* Lord Denning MR; *MBPXL Corp* v. *Intercontinental Banking
Corp*, 1975 CAT 411; reasonable evidence of future assets may be
sufficient—*Cybil Inc of Panama* v. *Timpuship*, 1978 CAT 478, and see Chap-
ter 4 p. 38.
[26] [1979] AC 210, HL (Kerr J, 20 December 1976; CA 1 June 1977—Lord
Denning MR, Lawton and Bridge L JJ; HL 26 October 1977—Lord Diplock,
Lord Hailsham, Lord Simon of Glaisdale, Lord Russell of Killowen, Lord
Keith of Kinkel); the decision will now be different because of the 1968
Brussels Convention, but the principles are valid.

vessel left Limassol in ballast. This was on 20 April 1976, and on 2 June 1976 she became a total loss after sinking off Greece. The *Siskina* was insured with London underwriters, and the shipowners claimed against them for the loss.

In the meantime, the Saudi Arabian cargo owners had heard of the arrest of their goods in Cyprus, and tried to arrange a release. Some cargo was given up on payment of a proportion of the charter freight, and other cargo owners applied for release through the courts in Cyprus, making a claim for damages against the shipowners at the same time. It was understood, however, that the shipowners had no assets except the insurance proceeds on the *Siskina*, which were payable in London.

Consequently, the cargo owners started proceedings in London on 2 July 1976, claiming damages for breach of contract and breach of duty on the part of the shipowners, and asking for a *Mareva* over the insurance proceeds. Mocatta J gave this order, as well as leave under Order 11, *ex parte*. Kerr J, however, set aside the Order 11 leave, and continued the injunction only until appeal. The Court of Appeal held that the plaintiffs were entitled to Order 11 leave and an injunction, but the House of Lords decided that, because there was no invasion of a legal or equitable right in England, and the shipowners had not consented to the jurisdiction of the English courts, there was no consequential jurisdiction to grant an injunction.

This was a landmark decision. First, it made clear that the presence of money or assets here did not itself give jurisdiction to the courts, unlike the presence of a ship or aircraft for an *in rem* action.

Secondly, it was confirmed that an injunction cannot stand alone under Order 11,[27] but had to be linked to substantive relief within the order, despite the objective merits of the plaintiffs' case. Otherwise, as Lord Diplock said,[28] it would be an attempt to pull oneself up by one's own bootstraps. This was consistent with the principle that the High

---

[27] Then Order 11, r.1(1)(*i*), now Order 11, r.1(1)(*b*); see also *Rosler* v. *Hilbery* [1925] Ch 250 at pp. 258, 261 and 262.
[28] [1979] AC 210 at p. 257, B.

court could not grant an injunction unless it were in support of a legal or equitable interest.[29]

Thirdly, the *Mareva* injunction itself was not challenged or adversely commented upon.[30]

The Siskina therefore defined the bounds of the *Mareva* injunction. As such, it is a valuable decision because it has allowed the *Mareva* itself to flourish within those limits, always subject to the need for a legal or equitable right as its foundation. In view of the refusal of the House of Lords to reverse the *Mareva* cases (although they could still take that course, however unlikely), and following on its statutory support in the Supreme Court Act 1981,[31] and its clear recognition in the rules of the Supreme Court,[32] there cannot be any real doubt as to the power of the High Court to grant *Marevas*. The next chapter examines the procedure for such a grant, and the general principles of law involved.

---

[29] *Ibid*, at p. 256, E–F *per* Lord Diplock, and see discussion above.
[30] See p. 254, C–E *per* Lord Diplock, and p. 261, E *per* Lord Hailsham; this implied acceptance was taken as approval by Lord Denning MR in *Third Chandris* [1979] 1 QB 645, at pp. 666–667, and see Griffiths L J in *AJ Bekhor & Co Ltd* v. *Bilton* [1981] 1 QB 923, CA at p. 947 F–G.
[31] Section 37, see p. 10.
[32] Order 29, r.1, see p. 33.

CHAPTER 4

Application for a "Mareva"

In the previous three chapters we have considered the background to the *Mareva*. It is now necessary to look at the factors present when making an application.

A *Mareva* injunction is sought because the plaintiff fears the consequences of not restraining the defendant. Thus, in whichever court the application is made, it is usually *ex parte* on affidavit, and can be before issue of the writ or originating summons in urgent cases, so long as the order contains an undertaking to issue forthwith.[1] It is an application in chambers except in the Chancery Division.[1a]

Order 29, r.1 provides:

(1) An application for the grant of an injunction may be made by any party to a cause or matter before or after trial of the cause or matter, whether or not a claim for the injunction was included in that party's writ, originating summons, counterclaim or third party notice, as the case may be.

(2) Where the applicant is the plaintiff and the case is one of urgency such application may be made *ex parte* on affidavit but, except as aforesaid, such application must be made by motion or summons.

(3) The plaintiff may not make such an application before the issue of the writ or originating summons by which the cause or matter is to be begun except where the case is one of urgency, and in that case the injunction applied for may be granted on terms providing for the issue of the writ or summons and such other terms, if any, as the court thinks fit.

In *Refson & Co Ltd* v. *Saggers and another*[2] it was said that the court should see either the engrossed writ or a draft, or if the application was by telephone counsel should read the relevant parts to the judge. Also, the term "forthwith" was preferable to "as soon as practicable" or similar

[1] *Re N (Infants)* [1967] Ch 512, see pp. 527–8.
[1a] When it is usually in *camera*.
[2] [1984] 1 WLR 1025, Ch D, Nourse J.

phrases, so that the undertaking, as an example, would be: ". . . forthwith to issue a writ of summons in the form of the said draft writ . . ." or some closely similar term. If necessary, counsel should remind his instructing solicitor to have the writ issued because of the contempt consequences of breaking the undertaking.

Although most *Mareva* applications are in the Commercial Court[3] the principles are the same wherever the order is granted. Thus, an applicant must put the writ or a draft before the court, together with an affidavit (in draft if absolutely unavoidable) setting out the claim, the amount, and the points, if any, made against it by the defendant. The addition of a statement or points of claim is helpful because it outlines in proper pleadings the plaintiff's case.

The affidavit must also show that it is reasonable to believe that there are assets of the defendant within the jurisdiction, and that there is a real risk that the defendant will make himself judgment-proof by deliberately dealing with them unless restrained. Further, full and frank disclosure of all material matters must be made, putting in more than is necessary in preference to making omissions which are later seen as relevant.[4] The affidavit can be sworn by an individual plaintiff, a senior officer or director of a plaintiff corporation, or the plaintiff's solicitor in control of the action. An undertaking to swear an affidavit put forward in draft must be included in the injunction. If necessary, confidentiality can be maintained by the use of initials instead of full titles in the case headings.

---

[3] Order 72, r.2: "commercial action" includes any cause arising out of the ordinary transactions of merchants and traders and, without prejudice to the generality of the foregoing words, any cause relating to the construction of a mercantile document, the export or import of merchandise, affreightment, insurance, banking, mercantile agency and mercantile usage; if the action is commercial but started outside the Commercial List an application to transfer should be made, under Order 72, r.5; see generally Colman, *The Practice and Procedure of the Commercial Court* (London: Lloyd's of London Press Ltd, 1983). Commercial Court office telephone number: 01–936 6826.

[4] *The Assios* [1979] 1 Lloyd's Rep. 337, where the activities of the plaintiffs were condemned as an attempt to trap the defendants; information apparently so sensitive and confidential that it could not be used at trial should not be put before the court on an *ex parte* application—*WEA Records Ltd* v. *Visions Channel 4 Ltd and others* [1983] 1 WLR 721, CA, especially Sir John Donaldson MR at p. 724.

A draft order, usually settled by counsel, must include all the terms of the injunction applied for, together with the undertakings, and should be added to the bundle containing the writ and affidavit, which are generally delivered to the court before the hearing.[5] Oral argument on the basis of the documents can then take place, and if the application is successful the draft order, with any amendments, will be initialled by the judge and is immediately operative.[6]

Notice can therefore be given to the defendant and third parties in control of assets, by telephone if necessary, and the written order will be sent on. This should contain a penal notice warning of the consequences of a breach of the injunction. Costs on an *ex parte* application are usually in cause.

Provision can be made in the order for an individual defendant within the jurisdiction to draw a certain amount of money as reasonable living expenses, but the usual course is for the defendant to apply to the court for such a variation.

The *Mareva* may state a specific sum which is frozen, or may simply be an overall order covering all the defendant's assets, which will also lead to an application to discharge or vary. The purpose of a specific maximum sum is to allow the defendant the use of the balance of his assets, but the application of a maximum to third parties who have no knowledge of what other assets are held by or for the defendant can cause problems, because of the danger that any release of funds or assets in the belief that other assets are frozen will possibly be in breach of the order. The solution is for an order for discovery to be made, to pinpoint and identify all the defendant's assets, so that those above the claim can be released. The maximum sum can, it is submitted, not only cover the amount claimed, but costs, together with interest, and the likely damages and costs incurred for third parties.

Undertaking as to damages and third party costs

The undertaking given by a plaintiff as to damages and third party costs may be underwritten by security or a bond,

[5] See *Practice Direction (Judge in Chambers: Procedure)* [1983] 1 WLR 433, at p. 434 for *ex parte* QBD applications.
[6] Appendix I for draft orders.

to provide assurance of some financial redress, but this is not a pre-condition to the grant of a *Mareva*. Further, the fact that a plaintiff is legally aided and therefore has no means to pay a defendant if the injunction is discharged and an inquiry as to damages decides that the plaintiff is liable, is not relevant to the application, nor to its effect against third parties.[7]

The fact that third party costs will increase the more that they have to do is an incentive to make the order as clear and specific as possible. Although the defendant will be ordered to pay the plaintiff's costs in most cases if the plaintiff succeeds, these will be taxed and may not represent the plaintiff's indemnity to third parties in full. Also, the defendant's assets may be insufficient, and reliance on his liability to pay is unwise.

The claim

The plaintiff does not have to have a strong *prima facie* case, nor one which will succeed in Order 14 proceedings. Rather, the test is now whether he has a good arguable claim, coupled with the court's discretion in any particular case. As was stated in the *Ninemia* case[8]:

> A "good arguable case" is no doubt the minimum which the plaintiff must show in order to cross what the judge rightly described as the "threshold" for the exercise of the jurisdiction. But at the end of the day the court must consider the evidence as a whole in deciding whether or not to exercise this statutory jurisdiction.

Risk

The present position as to risk, after many different interpretations by practitioners and others, is noted in *Ninemia* as follows[9]:

[7] *Allen and others* v. *Jambo Holdings Ltd and others* [1981] 1 WLR 1251, CA.

[8] [1983] 1 WLR 1412, CA, at p. 1417; contrast e.g. *J T Stratford & Sons Ltd* v. *Lindly* [1965] AC 629.

[9] [1983] 1 WLR 1412, CA, at p. 1422.

... the test is whether, on the assumption that the plaintiffs have shown at least "a good arguable case", the court concludes, on the whole of the evidence then before it, that the refusal of a *Mareva* injunction would involve a real risk that a judgment or award in favour of the plaintiffs would remain unsatisfied.

Many factors go to make up risk. The fact that a company is incorporated in a financial or tax haven overseas might be relevant, as is its trading history and that of its personnel, especially its directing minds. Its activities and the kind of business it is in are important. Financial data is useful in assessing the risk, especially if it can be argued that apparently sound accounts are based on artificial inflation, such as the cross-firing of money between linked accounts to create the impression of a solid turnover. In essence, does the defendant have any characteristics which suggest he can and will frustrate judgment? In all respects it is a question of seeking information and analysing it. In many ways the principle of whether a defendant is likely to snap his fingers[10] at the court is as good a test as any. Thus, if a defendant is likely to behave in that manner, and it is possible to produce evidence to that effect to the court, an injunction is more likely than not.

As Lawton L J stated in *Third Chandris*[11]:

There must be facts from which the Commercial Court, like a prudent, sensible commercial man, can properly infer a danger of default ... For commercial men, when assessing risks, there is no commercial equivalent of the Criminal Records Office or Ruff's Guide to the Turf. What they have to do is to find out all they can about the party with whom they are dealing, including origins, business domicile, length of time in business, assets and the like; and they will probably be wary of the appearances of wealth which are not backed up by known assets. In my judgment the Commercial Court should approve applications for *Mareva* injunctions in the same way. Its judges have special experience of commercial cases and they can be expected to identify likely debt dodgers as well

[10] *Per* Kerr J, mentioned by Lord Denning MR in *Pertamina* [1978] 1 QB 644, CA, at p. 661.
[11] [1979] 1 QB 645, CA, at p. 671.

as, probably better than, most businessmen. They should not expect to be given proof of previous defaults or specific incidents of commercial malpractice.

It was also observed that the absence of any available information about the defendant, so long as a thorough search had been made, was itself probably suspicious.

Assets

The *Mareva* applies to all assets tangible and intangible within the jurisdiction, but not those outside.[12] It covers land,[13] motor-cars and other chattels,[14] bank accounts, ships and aircraft (see below), and even goodwill.[15] In short, subject to the wording of the order, all assets are potentially within the scope of the *Mareva*, so long as they are in the jurisdiction and in the legal or beneficial ownership of the defendant, and are not subject to legal or equitable interests of third parties. Thus, a third party in possession of goods under a contract with the defendant cannot be denied his rights because of the *Mareva*. The test must be whether the assets will be available on execution of a judgment, and if they are they can be the subject of the *Mareva*, as its purpose is to aid the court's process. It would otherwise be illogical to include them in the order. Money in a joint bank account must be expressly included, or else it will not be covered. Further, the plaintiff cannot freeze assets held by the defendant in another capacity other than that of defendant, by analogy with garnishee proceedings.[16]

It is to be noted that the value of the assets for the *Mareva* is seen from the plaintiff's point of view, and not the defendant's, so that if the benefit to the plaintiff is small compared

[12] *Intraco Ltd* v. *Notis Shipping Corp of Liberia* [1981] 2 Lloyd's Rep. 256, CA, and see p. 30, note 25.
[13] E.g. *Kirby* v. *Banks*, 1980 CAT 624; *Praznovsky* v. *Sablyack* [1977] VR 114.
[14] E.g. *CBS United Kingdom Ltd* v. *Lambert and another* [1983] Ch 37, CA.
[15] *Darashah* v. *UFAC (UK) Ltd, The Times*, 30 March 1982, CA.
[16] *Roberts* v. *Death* (1881) 8 QBD 319.

to the loss to the defendant, the injunction will not be granted. In *Pertamina*[17] the value of goods seized was only $350,000 to the plaintiff, as scrap, but their value to the defendant was $12 million. The scrap value was considered comparatively trifling, and was one of the major reasons for not granting a *Mareva*.

Ships and aircraft

Marevas are as applicable to ships and aircraft as they are to other assets. In *Allen and others* v. *Jambo Holdings Ltd and others*[18] a claim for personal injuries was likely to be made, and counsel telephoned Drake J and obtained a *Mareva* injunction as a matter of urgency, to restrain a Nigerian company and its pilot from removing an aircraft from the jurisdiction, so that it could be retained pending the litigation, or the provision of security. In the Court of Appeal this use of a *Mareva* was approved. In a later unreported case *Visionair International Inc* v. *Euroworld California Inc*[19] three DC3 aircraft at Exeter airport were the subject of a *Mareva*, although the order was discharged for other reasons. There is authority therefore for the continued application of restraining orders against aircraft, probably even when alternative proceedings can be started under the Admiralty jurisdiction of the High Court.[20] The practical result is the same because a breach of either is contempt, but the benefits of speed with a *Mareva* must be balanced against the absence of any statutory lien as would result under the Admiralty jurisdiction.

Marevas are equally applicable to ships, even though this is an area where the Admiralty jurisdiction is paramount. Clearly, in cases not coming within the heads of claim in section 20 of the Supreme Court Act 1981 there is no doubt

[17] [1978] 1 QB 644, CA.
[18] [1980] 1 WLR 1251, CA (20 July 1979).
[19] 1979 CAT 719 (30 November 1979), on appeal from Reeve J—Exeter District Registry, and from Mustill J—QBD Comm. Ct.
[20] Supreme Court Act 1981, ss.20, 21. Admiralty actions against aircraft are rare, but see *Re the Glider Standard Austria SA* [1965] P 463.

a *Mareva* can be applied for. In *Gatoil Industries Inc* v. *Arkwright Boston Manufacturers Mutual Insurance Co*[21] it was held that a dispute over insurance premiums was not sufficiently connected with the carriage of goods to come within the Scottish Admiralty jurisdiction, but there seems no reason why, if the facts had been repeated in England, a *Mareva* could not have been granted. If otherwise, the ship is neither arrestable nor subject to the same restraint as other assets, and this would be illogical. On the other hand, should a *Mareva* be granted when relief is possible within the Admiralty jurisdiction? If the applicant is prepared to take what is essentially a lesser interim relief, there seems to be no reason why he could not do so, as the result is no more harmful to the shipowner and less beneficial to the applicant, except where the court restrains more than one ship. In *The Rena K*[22] it was said that the prospect of a plaintiff having cumulative kinds of security for any one claim was not objectionable, and this view must, it is submitted, be correct. There is no good reason to exclude ships and aircraft from the *Mareva* jurisdiction, nor to force a plaintiff to seek one remedy rather than another.

The particular problems of banks

The compliance by banks with a *Mareva* is acknowledged as expensive and time-consuming.[23] Thus, the order as it relates to them should identify clearly, on the *ex parte* hearing, what assets are covered and to what extent. It is not correct to have a wide order at the outset on the grounds that a later hearing can tighten it up.

It ought to be possible to identify money within the jurisdiction, and say which banks hold it and at which branches.

---

[21] [1985] 2 WLR 74, HL (Sc).

[22] [1979] 1 QB 377, Brandon J; in *Sanko Steamship Co Ltd* v. *DC Commodities (Australasia) Pty Ltd* [1980] WAR 51, the *Mareva* covered ship's bunkers, see also *Clipper Maritime Co Ltd of Monrovia* v. *Mineralimportexport* [1981] 1 WLR 1262.

[23] *Z Ltd* v. *A-Z and AA-LL* [1982] 1 QB 558, CA, especially Kerr L J at pp. 585–593; *Searose Ltd* v. *Seatrain UK Ltd* [1981] 1 WLR 894, at p. 897.

The number and type of account is also important. The more information that is available will reduce the costs of carrying out the order, which are the responsibility of the plaintiff.

One further problem is the application of the *Mareva* to assets other than money held by the bank. It was suggested by Kerr L J[24] that shares, title deeds, or articles held in safe custody by the bank are either not covered unless specifically referred to in the order, or perhaps should generally be expressly excluded. With respect, the injunction should expressly exclude them if necessary because otherwise they, being assets of the defendant, cannot be moved at all if an overall order is granted, and not until some value has been ascertained if a maximum sum order is used. The best course in the latter case is to order the defendant to swear an affidavit listing his assets and their value. In the meantime they must be covered by the order.

If accounts are held in a currency other than the one in the order it is probably best for the sums in the account to be converted to the currency of the order, so that like can be compared with like.

In conclusion, the best way to avoid problems with banks and other third parties is to make the terms of the order as clear and as specific as possible at the outset.

"Marevas" and arbitration

The High Court has power under section 12(6) of the Arbitration Act 1950 to grant interim relief where the dispute is either referable to arbitration or has already been so referred. The injunction can additionally contain an undertaking or term that the arbitration will be started within a certain time, or that the injunction will continue until a certain date after the award.[25] This is clear from the judgment of Brandon J in *The Rena K*,[26] where section 12(6)(*f*),

[24] At p. 590 H.
[25] E.g. *Cretanor Maritime Co Ltd* v. *Irish Marine Management Ltd* [1978] 1 WLR 966, CA.
[26] [1979] 1 QB 377, especially p. 408.

securing the amount in dispute in the reference, and section 12(6)(*h*), interim injunctions or the appointment of a receiver, were specifically considered.

The grant of a *Mareva* is possible notwithstanding that one party can apply to the court for a stay of litigation pending the reference, because the court is not hearing the dispute itself, but exercising its jurisdiction as to interim measures. There is nothing inconsistent with parties agreeing to refer disputes to arbitration, but being subject to the interim powers of the courts,[27] and standard arbitration rules provide for this.[28]

In practice, the applicant for a *Mareva* still has to show that there are assets in the jurisdiction, and this may be difficult in arbitration references because of the popularity of London as an arbitration forum, without any other direct connection between the parties in many cases.

Family Division

The clear and experienced practice of the Family Division in granting injunctions to safeguard matrimonial assets (for example the net proceeds of sale of the matrimonial home, its contents, and bank accounts) pending proceedings for financial relief, under section 37 of the Matrimonial Causes Act 1973,[29] avoids the need for many *Mareva* applications, but in some instances the *Mareva* relief is useful, especially where proceedings have not yet started and urgent relief is required, because an application can be made to a judge of the High Court immediately, rather than through the Registrar as provided for in standard safeguarding applications. Also, the principles of discovery appropriate to a *Mareva* may be called in aid when the rules do not otherwise provide a remedy. Consequently, the *Mareva* has a role to play, albeit limited by the existence of a fairly wide and reasonably strong specific statutory power.

[27] The dispute in *The Mareva* [1975] 2 Lloyd's Rep. 509, CA, was *prima facie* referable to arbitration, see Roskill L J at p. 512.

[28] E.g. UNCITRAL Arbitration Rules, Art. 26(3); ICC Rules, Art. 8(5).

[29] See Matrimonial Causes Rules (1977), r.84; Chapter 2 p. 17 *et seq.*

The County Court

The County Court has jurisdiction within its financial limits to grant a *Mareva* injunction in the same way as the High Court,[30] but only where the injunction is ancillary to a claim for money or other relief.[31] It need not be a substantial, nor the primary, claim, because it is not appropriate for the court to decide at the interlocutory stage whether one claim or another is the primary one, but it must be bona fide.[32]

The present financial limits are up to £5,000 for claims in tort and contract, to £1,000 annual rateable value for land, to £30,000 for Chancery matters and for claims under the Inheritance (Provision for Family and Dependants) Act 1975. There is also the same jurisdiction to grant an injunction and a declaration relating to land as the High Court.[33]

Marevas are not common in the County Court, but are occasionally applied for and granted, especially when information comes to light on discovery which indicates a risk of dissipation or removal of assets. The greatest drawback to fuller use of the County Court is the financial limit on jurisdiction, but *Marevas* are just as vital in appropriate cases as in other courts, and in some cases more so because of the disproportionate effect on an individual plaintiff of losing his chance to enforce a County Court judgment.

"Marevas" to aid execution

A *Mareva* may be granted in aid of execution[34] on the same basis as in an application before judgment, except that the

[30] County Courts Act 1984, ss.38, 39; Order 13, r.6 CCR; Order 29, r.1 CCR—contempt of court.

[31] *R* v. *Cheshire County Court Judge and National Soc of Boilermakers, ex parte Malone* [1921] 2 KB 694.

[32] E.g. *Hatt & Co (Bath) Ltd* v. *Pearce* [1978] 1 WLR 885, CA—claim for £1 damages; *Ambridge (Reading) Ltd* v. *Hedges*, 1972 CAT 74.

[33] County Courts Act 1984, s.22.

[34] *Orwell Steel (Erection & Fabrication) Ltd* v. *Asphalt & Tarmac (UK) Ltd* [1984] 1 WLR 1097, Farquharson J; *Hill Samuel & Co Ltd* v. *Littauer* (5 December 1984) QBD Comm Ct, Bingham J; *Stewart Chartering Ltd* v. *C & O Managements SA* [1980] 1 WLR 460, QDB Comm Ct, Goff J— *Mareva* continued after judgment.

existence of the judgment itself provides the basis of the claim. Risk must still be proved.

This power is exercisable despite the existence of other methods for enforcing execution, and it is for the judgment creditor to take his remedies as he wishes to apply them. The key issue to consider is whether the *Mareva* is in aid of the procedure of the court, but it must be remembered from the judgment creditor's point of view that the *Mareva* gives no rights in the property, unlike other methods in the execution process.

Further scope

Although this book proceeds on the basis that the plaintiff in an action applies for a *Mareva*, there is no reason why a defendant could not do so, so long as he can satisfy the tests of a good arguable claim and risk. Although it is hard to see how a defendant against whom a *Mareva* has been granted can himself seek a *Mareva* against a plaintiff, there is no bar against him seeking one against a third party upon whom, for example, he is to serve a third party notice. Also, if the defendant fears that a plaintiff in an action not including a *Mareva* will not be good for a counterclaim, he can again apply for an order against him. The same would be the case if a defendant without a counterclaim is seriously concerned that on a reasonable expectation of winning his case, the plaintiff will frustrate an order for costs in the defendant's favour.

Additionally, a party seeking redress in one of the statutory tribunals, such as an industrial tribunal, should be able to seek a *Mareva* from the High Court if it is otherwise appropriate, for example if an employer who is sued for unfair dismissal is about to make himself judgment-proof.

Further, the *Mareva* in aid of execution of foreign judgments and awards is a logical extension, already envisaged by its potential use in restraining a defendant's assets here while litigation is pending in the EEC, as will be discussed in Chapter 10.

Although limited in extent by practical reasons, there is no limit to the High Court's jurisdiction within the objectively strict guidelines so far discussed, starting as they do with jurisdiction, and resting securely on the twin tests of a good arguable case and risk.

CHAPTER 5

Appeals, and applications to discharge and vary

The *Mareva* injunction is almost always obtained *ex parte*, and often before issue and service of the writ. Therefore, there is no opportunity to test the defendant's reaction to such an order before it is granted, and although the majority of *Marevas* are unopposed at any stage of the proceedings, a significant minority involve later *inter partes* hearings, and some cases go to appeal.

Ex parte orders of any nature are essentially provisional because the judge making them has only heard submissions and seen evidence from one party, and although there is a heavy burden on counsel to make full and fair disclosure of all information in his possession, it is only on an *inter partes* hearing that the true risk, as well as factors influencing the size or validity of the main claim, can be properly assessed.

The *inter partes* hearing is sometimes before the same judge who granted the order *ex parte*, but in practice, especially for urgent cases, another judge will hear the case because the first is busy. The *inter partes* hearing is not an appeal, but an opportunity for both sides to be heard before a decision is taken on the original order. As Sir John Donaldson MR said in *WEA Records Ltd* v. *Visions Channel 4 Ltd and others*[1]:

> He expects at a later stage to be given an opportunity to review his provisional order in the light of evidence and argument adduced by the other side and, in so doing, he is not hearing an appeal from himself and in no way feels inhibited from discharging or varying his original order.

The same sentiments apply of course to other judges in the same matter.

[1] [1983] 1 WLR 721, CA, at p. 727, E.

In fact, an *inter partes* hearing may not be necessary because the defendant may be prepared to offer security, or to give an undertaking to the court which will satisfy the plaintiff. Quite often, for example, a sum of money can be placed on joint deposit by the defendant in the names of himself and the plaintiff, and an undertaking to the court to do so will move the plaintiff to accept that the injunction should be discharged. It must be emphasized, however, that it is for the court to discharge the order it has made, and formal approval has to be sought and obtained. If the undertaking is acceptable, the defendant should repeat it to the court, whereupon he becomes bound by it as much as by an injunction, in so far as breach of it is still contempt.[2] If, on the other hand, he provides adequate security for the plaintiff, or indeed settles the plaintiff's claim, it is submitted that no attendance on the defendant's part is needed as the plaintiff can apply *ex parte*, on notice, for the injunction to be discharged, giving all the relevant reasons. Indeed, an application on documents alone may be made in straightforward circumstances, thus saving the expense of an oral hearing. The court will require evidence that no third party served with the order has suffered any damages that need to be assessed and awarded.

For other cases the defendant will either make no appearance or will challenge the order. In the latter case, he will either seek to discharge or vary the injunction, which he can do on a variety of bases. It is preferable for a defendant to answer the plaintiff's pleadings with his own before making an application, unless the statement or points of claim have not yet been served.

The good arguable claim

First of all a defendant can seek to show that the plaintiff does not have a good arguable claim. If he does so successfully the twin test of the *Mareva* cannot be satisfied and it should be discharged. Such a simple discharge is very rare

---

[2] *Milburn* v. *Newton Colliery Ltd* (1908) 52 SJ 317; Chapter 9, p. 101.

because of the guidelines originally applied by the courts in the *ex parte* hearing.

Reduction of the "Mareva" sum by set-off

In many cases the possibility exists of reducing the sum frozen by establishing a good arguable counterclaim or set-off. If, for example, a plaintiff obtains a *Mareva* for £1 million, and the defendant has a good arguable counterclaim for £750,000, why should he not seek to have the *Mareva* sum reduced to the balance of the two competing claims, that is £250,000? After all, if the same test is applied to both parties, the *prima facie* claims will have been judged on the same basis, and it would only be fair and equitable to reduce the sums accordingly.

There is an even stronger case for reducing the *Mareva* sum where a pure set-off exists, because this is a defence to the claim enjoying a right of being pleaded as such.[3]

The instances giving rise to a reduction can appear in many ways. For example, a plaintiff suing his agent for the full proceeds of sales could be met by a reduction to take into account commission due, or agreed expenses. There might be a contractual right to deduct mony from invoices for late delivery of goods, or a term in a lease for withholding or reducing rent on the failure of a landlord to provide full services to his tenants. Contractual set-offs are straightforward and should cause no problem in an application to vary, especially as the existence of the right is something which should, perhaps, have been disclosed previously. In other cases it must be for the court to assess how the sum sought to be set-off matches in with the plaintiff's claim. For instance, a debtor can generally set off a liquidated claim of his against a liquidated claim by his creditor, even if arising out of separate contracts. If the claim is unliquidated it can be pleaded against a liquidated or unliquidated claim if both arise out of the same or a connected contract.[4]

---

[3] Order 18, r.7; Supreme Court Act 1981, s.49(2)(a).
[4] *Hanak* v. *Green* [1958] 2 QB 9; also *Bankes* v. *Jarvis* [1903] 1 KB 549; *BICC PLC* v. *Bundy & Co and others* [1985] 2 WLR 132, CA.

Lord Hanworth MR said, in *In re a Bankruptcy Notice*[5]:

> ("set-off") is a word well known and established in its meaning; it is something which provides a defence because the nature and quality of the sum so relied upon are such that it is a sum which is proper to be dealt with as diminishing the claim which is made, and against which the sum so demanded can be set off.

The defence of set-off can arise in many *Mareva* cases, and in general it has been accepted in appropriate circumstances, although not as yet in clear terms in any reported cases.[6] Except in debt-collecting actions where the *Mareva* is a precaution only against the delay inherent in summary proceedings, the opportunity of a set-off is an important one and can be used to advantage.

Lack of full disclosure

There is a powerful argument in the view that if full and frank disclosure has not been made in the *ex parte* application, the order will be discharged because of the seriousness of the omission. This is because it is up to the judge to consider the importance of the relevant facts, so that he can exercise his discretion in the light of as much information as possible. Consequently, a lack of full and frank disclosure need not be deliberate before the injunction is discharged for that reason, but merely has to be pertinent to the issues involved, even if it does not affect the merits of the claim.[7]

---

[5] [1934] Ch 431, at p. 437.

[6] In *Pac-Asian Services Pte Ltd* v. *Steladean*, QBD Comm Ct, Staughton J (15 December 1983) a counterclaim was set off against the claim to arrive at a net figure for the purposes of the injunction, to which was added an estimated figure for interest and costs; in *Continental Airlines Inc* v. *Aviation & Tourist Marketing AG* QBD Comm Ct, Webster J (18 January 1984) it was a net figure after considering claims and counterclaims which was used by the court, although the injunction was in fact discharged; *Fary-Jones (Insurance) Ltd* v. *IFM Funding GmbH*, 1979 CAT 223 also appears to approve a final sum being used by Slade J, after taking into account all facts on the claims.

[7] See e.g. *Thermax Ltd* v. *Schott Industrial Glass Ltd* [1981] FSR 289.

No evidence of risk

It must be clear from the plaintiff's affidavit served with the order that there is evidence of risk. Although this evidence can be supplemented by persuasive argument by counsel, the evidence itself must be in the affidavit, at the very minimum by showing clear grounds of fear of dissipation or removal. As it is not open to a plaintiff simply to say "I fear", the absence of real evidence is a weak point to attack strongly, in the unlikely event that a *Mareva* has been granted on that basis.

It is far more common for facts to have been used in such a way as to indicate risk, when actually there can be a logical or at least reasonable explanation for them. It is thus open to the defendant to serve an affidavit in reply, containing sufficient details and exhibits to back up the contention that there is no risk. Above all, the defendant's legal advisers must have as much information as is necessary in their opinion to conduct the case properly.[8] Advocacy on its own cannot compensate for real information, especially when the plaintiff is in the comparatively strong position of passing the burden on to the defendant to show why the injunction should be discharged.

Variation of order in favour of third parties

It is often the case that a third party affected by a *Mareva* blocking the defendant's money or assets will intervene in the *inter partes* hearing, or will apply alone to have the injunction varied or discharged.[9] The courts are reluctant to allow injunctions to interfere with the rights of third parties, and on reasonable evidence will allow variations. For example, in *Galaxia Maritime SA* v. *Mineralimportexport*[10]

---

[8] See observations by Lord Denning MR in *Third Chandris* [1979] 1 QB 645, CA, at pp. 664–666.

[9] Provision is made in the rules for intervention (e.g. Order 15, r.6(2)(*b*)), and in the practice of the Commercial Court.

[10] [1982] 1 WLR 539, CA (18 December 1981—the day after *Z Ltd* v. *A-Z and AA-LL* was decided by the court).

the owners of a vessel which had on board a cargo belonging to the defendants, whose assets had been frozen by a *Mareva* on 16 December 1981, applied to have the order discharged on 17 December 1981 so that the vessel could sail. The alternative was a denial to the shipowners of the use of their only trading asset, in a dispute which was none of their real concern. Despite an undertaking on the plaintiff's part to pay the reasonable costs of third parties inconvenienced by the order, it was held that the *Mareva* should be discharged. Eveleigh L J said[11]:

> A third party is entitled to freedom of action and he is entitled to trade freely. I do not think that a plaintiff has the right to a "compulsory purchase" of the rights of a third party and that is what it amounts to in this case.

Kerr L J put the same view in equally strong terms[12]:

> ... it is crucial to bear in mind not only the balance of convenience and justice as between plaintiffs and defendants, but above all also as between plaintiffs and third parties. Where assets of a defendant are held by a third party incidentally to the general business of the third party—such as the accounts of the defendant held by a bank, or goods held by a bailee as custodian, for example in a warehouse—an effective indemnity in favour of the third party will adequately hold this balance, because service of the injunction will not lead to any major interference with the third party's business. But where the effect of service must lead to interference with the performance of a contract between the third party and the defendant which relates specifically to the assets in question, the right of the third party in relation to his contract must clearly prevail over the plaintiff's desire to secure the defendant's assets for himself against the day of judgment.

Thus it may be said that whenever an injunction involves a substantial and unwarrantable interference with the trading activity of third parties, except for those whose business it is to hold money or goods to someone's account, the rights of the third party will overcome the plaintiff's rights

---

[11] At p. 541, G–H.
[12] At p. 542, E–G; Sir George Baker fully agreed with the reasons for allowing the appeal.

to have a *Mareva* for protecting an eventual judgment. In fact, a subsidiary factor in the *Galaxia* case was the interference the injunction would have caused to the Christmas holiday arrangements of the ship's crew, and this sort of factor is relevant in cases involving the employment of staff by third parties when the order dislocates their work.

In some cases, however, the position of third parties can be dealt with by an undertaking or proviso in the order. Thus, in *Clipper Maritime Co Ltd of Monrovia* v. *Mineralimportexport*[13] the plaintiffs obtained a *Mareva* against the defendant's cargo. The effect of the order was again to prevent the vessel leaving port, and because this was an interference with the administration of the port, the plaintiffs had to give an undertaking to reimburse the port authority for the income lost by the continued presence of the ship. The order also contained a proviso allowing the authority to move the vessel around in the port for operational reasons, and if necessary to move her out of the port anywhere within the High Court's jurisdiction. These conditions were imposed after representations to the court by solicitors representing the British Ports Association, and Goff J went on to say[14]:

> It is, therefore, of great assistance if the court can be kept informed of any adverse effect which these injunctions are having upon third parties, as in the case of the clearing banks and port authorities, so that steps can be taken where possible to protect their interests. If any other bodies wish to make representations on this point, it would be most appropriate for them to address their representations to the secretary of the Commercial Court Committee at the Royal Courts of Justice, in which event they will immediately be drawn to the attention of the judge in charge of the Commercial List.

A defendant may also wish to pay debts due to third parties. The proper course is for him to apply to do so, but a third party is equally entitled to intervene and ask for a variation of the order to permit such payments to be made.[15]

---

[13] [1981] 1 WLR 1262, Goff J.
[14] At p. 1264.
[15] E.g. *A* v. *B (X intervening)* [1983] 2 Lloyd's Rep. 532, QBD Comm Ct, Parker J; *Bakarim* v. *Victoria P Shipping Co Ltd, The Tatiangela* [1980] 2 Lloyd's Rep. 193, QBD Comm Ct, Parker J.

The principles on which he does so are the same as on a defendant's application to pay these debts.

Variation to enable payments to be made

A defendant is *prima facie* entitled to pay normal debts arising in the course of business, so long as the policy behind the *Mareva* is kept to. Thus, if a defendant puts sufficient evidence to the court of how the debt arose, including the circumstances of the defendant's dealings with the creditor, his invoice and if appropriate his final demand or letter before action, the variation will generally be allowed because the alternative is for the creditor to have to proceed to judgment and seize the assets covered by the *Mareva* up to his judgment debt. A judgment creditor has a greater right to the defendant's assets than someone with a mere restraining order, and to avoid the need to go to such lengths an approach should first be made to the plaintiff's solicitors to see if they will consent to a variation. If they do not do so, an application based on affidavit evidence can be made. In general terms it does not matter that the debt is legally unenforceable, if the defendant would be expected to pay it in his particular trade. In *Iraqi Ministry of Defence and others* v. *Arcepey Shipping Co SA (Gillespie Bros & Co Ltd intervening) (The Angel Bell)*, it was said[16]:

> A reputable businessman who has received a loan from another person is likely to regard it as dishonourable, if not dishonest, not to repay that loan even if the enforcement of the loan is technically illegal by virtue of the Moneylenders Acts. All the interveners are asking is that the defendants should be free to repay such a loan if they think fit to do so, not that the loan transaction should be enforced. For a defendant to be free to repay a loan in such circumstances is not inconsistent with the policy underlying the *Mareva* jurisdiction. He is not in such circumstances seeking to avoid his responsibilities to the plaintiff if the latter should ultimately

[16] [1980] 1 Lloyd's Rep. 632, QBD Comm Ct, Goff J. (13 November 1979), at p. 637.

obtain a judgment; on the contrary, he is seeking in good faith to make payments which he considers he should make in the ordinary course of business. I cannot see that the *Mareva* jurisdiction should be allowed to prevent such a payment. To allow it to do so would be to stretch it beyond its original purpose so that instead of preventing abuse it would rather prevent businessmen conducting their businesses as they are entitled to do.

Consequently, the applicant has to show that the payments are in good faith and in the ordinary course of business, and are not being made with the aim of reducing the assets available to the plaintiff.

A defendant must, nevertheless, show that he has no other funds from which the payments can be made. He cannot choose to reduce the funds frozen when he can meet his liabilities in other ways, and therefore applications from defendants will be refused if full disclosure of the financial position is not made.[17] Whether such disclosure must be made when an intervener alone applies will have to depend on the defendant's willingness to supply the information, and the circumstances of the case. Certainly, the requirement cannot be avoided by the device of a third party application, nor can the third party have the almost impossible burden of disclosing the defendant's financial means.

A complication arises if, on an application to use frozen money to pay debts or legal expenses, the plaintiff alleges that the money is impressed with a trust, or subject to his proprietary claim, so that he opposes not only because the total funds would be reduced, but because he claims that the money is clearly his, albeit before a judgment to that effect has been given.

In *PCW (Underwriting Agencies) Ltd* v. *Dixon and another*[18] an application to vary so that more generous living expenses could be paid was opposed because the plaintiffs argued that the defendant was trying to use other people's money. It was not clear, however, that the relevant

[17] *A and B* v. *C (No. 2)* [1981] 1 Lloyd's Rep. 559.
[18] [1983] 2 All ER 158, QBD, Comm Ct, Lloyd J (20 January 1983); see also *A* v. *C* [1981] QB 596.

funds were trust funds and this, combined with the importance of allowing the defendant to continue a reasonable
lifestyle, to pay his debts, and to defend himself, militated
against holding to the original *Mareva*. On appeal, it was
ordered[19] that the drawing of money should first be made
against funds indisputably the defendant's, and not
impressed with any equitable interest of the plaintiffs or
other persons, secondly against funds reasonably believed
to be free of such beneficial interest, and, thirdly, against
funds the defendant did not know were impressed with such
a beneficial interest. Further, the defendant was to replace
with his own money all funds later found to be withdrawn
when impressed with the beneficial interest of others, and
this replacement would be subject to the same equities as
the withdrawn amounts. The complication of this order was
justified in the circumstances and indicates a certain
flexibility in dealing with unusual situations.

Applications by third parties to clarify orders

The interference of a *Mareva* with the business of third parties is an acknowledged disadvantage.[20] The position of
banks as against account holders is particularly subject to
difficulties, but others may also be affected. In the same way
that third parties can intervene to seek authorization for
payments from a defendant's funds, so too can clarification
be sought to avoid a third party acting either in contempt
of court or in breach of his contractual obligations to the
defendant.

This can be helpful when accounts frozen by a plaintiff
have in fact little or no connection with the defendant, perhaps because of false information or an incorrect analysis
of financial data. Either the bank or the true account holder
can intervene to clarify the order, and the plaintiff's remedy
would have to be to seek an order for discovery against those
parties to establish a viable connection with the defendant.

---

[19] 28 January 1983, Sir John Donaldson MR, Fox L J, *The Times*, 4
February 1983.
[20] See fns. 10, 11, 12, above.

The simple allegation that an account is the defendant's is not enough when the account-holder is a third party, and there has to be evidence that it is held on the defendant's behalf or to his order. In the absence of this proof the injunction will be varied. One application which is no longer necessary (if the original *Mareva* has been drafted correctly) is by banks to confirm that they have a right to exercise a set-off of loans made by them to the defendant against the sums frozen by the order in their control. As a defendant can apply to pay his ordinary trade creditors or they can intervene and ask for authorization of payments, so too can banks, except that it may in fact be easier for a bank to show that repayment of a loan made by it is a payment in the ordinary way of business. Why, though, should banks be forced to make such applications, if it can be avoided? As a result of *Oceanica Castelana Armadora SA of Panama* v. *Mineralimportexport (Barclays Bank International intervening)*[21] it is now the practice to include a form of words to allow a bank its right of set-off against the defendant's funds for facilities granted before the date of the original *Mareva*.[22]

Interveners' costs

The intervention of innocent third parties in a *Mareva* case should not entail them in expense. Although the usual *Mareva* order contains an undertaking to pay the reasonable costs of third parties, it was not clear how these should be calculated, in view of the then current practice on taxation of costs. In *Project Development Co Ltd SA* v. *KMK Securities Ltd and others (Syndicate Bank Intervening)*[23] it was held that interveners should be entitled in the normal course of events to an indemnity for their expenses incurred on a successful application to vary, subject to the proviso that the cost could be established as reasonable. The order

---

[21] [1983] 1 WLR 1294, QBD Comm Ct, Lloyd J (27 January 1983).
[22] *Ibid*, p. 1302, and see Appendix I.
[23] [1982] 1 WLR 1470, QBD Comm Ct, Parker J (6 July 1982); Order 62, r.29.

for costs should therefore be the intervener's costs to be
taxed on a solicitor and own client basis, with the
qualification that the intervener has to establish that they
were reasonably incurred and reasonable in amount.

Appeals[24]

An applicant for a *Mareva ex parte* who fails in his request
can appeal to the Court of Appeal, without leave, against
the interlocutory decision. A defendant against whom an
order has been made in the High Court must go there to
apply for discharge or variation,[25] and, if unsuccessful, he
can then appeal, again without leave. The plaintiff can of
course appeal if the defendant is successful, and interveners
in an action have the same rights.

Appeals are heard in open court, unless there is a formal
request to have the hearing *in camera*, for which an
approach has to be made to the Registrar of Civil Appeals
who will ask the court for its view.[26]

The order appealed against can be stayed until the appeal
hearing, so that, for example, the discharge of an injunction
can be delayed until the Court of Appeal has an opportunity
to decide, thus maintaining the status quo in the meantime.[27]

Appeals can be arranged with great speed, in or out of
term time, subject to the case warranting an expedited hearing. In vacation, counsel has to certify the urgency of the
appeal before a hearing is arranged because judges have to
be contacted with a view to forming a court.

The new practice of skeleton arguments and other
reforms[28] has improved the flow of hearings, and parties now

[24] See generally Order. 59, and Supreme Court Act 1981, s.18(1)(*h*); the
Civil Appeals General Office is Room 246, RCJ, and the listing of appeals
and appointments is Room 249.
[25] *WEA Records Ltd* v. *Visions Channel 4 Ltd and others* [1983] 1 WLR
721, CA.
[26] And see Order 33, r.4.
[27] Order 59, r.13.
[28] *Practice Note (Court of Appeal—Skeleton Arguments)* [1983] 1 WLR
1055; *Practice Note (Court of Appeal—New Procedures)* [1982] 1 WLR 1312;
Practice Note (Court of Appeal—New Procedures) (No. 2)) [1983] 1 WLR 598;
Practice Directions (Court of Appeal—Dismissal of Appeal) [1983] 1 WLR
85.

wait for less time before an appeal, especially as *Mareva* appeals are usually to a two-judge court.

The speed with which interlocutory proceedings proceed to argument can often lead to evidence coming to light after the decision, but before an appeal hearing. In such circumstances new evidence can be put in so long as it could not have been obtained with reasonable diligence for use at the trial, and it would have had, if given, an important although not necessarily decisive influence on the case. It must also be apparently credible, though it need not be incontrovertible.[29]

Finally, it should be noted that the Court of Appeal rarely interferes with the exercise of a judge's discretion in *Marevas* and other discretionary orders, unless the proper tests were not applied, or the judge misdirected himself as to the law, or took into account irrelevant points, or failed to take account of matters which should have been noted.[30] The fact that the Court of Appeal would have come to a different conclusion is not of itself a reason to allow an appeal.

Inquiry as to damages

The usual *Mareva* Order contains a plaintiff's undertaking as to damages, both in favour of third parties and the defendant. (It is also quite common for a plaintiff to give a cross-undertaking as to damages when an injunction is replaced by a defendant's undertaking,[31] as the undertaking may itself hamper the defendant and cause him loss and expense.)

When an injunction is discharged, whether before or at trial[32] it is open to a party who has suffered loss from the imposition or operation of the order to seek an inquiry as to

---

[29] *Ladd* v. *Marshall* [1954] 1 WLR 1489, CA; *Skone* v. *Skone* [1971] 1 WLR 812, HL; *Langdale and another* v. *Danby* [1982] 1 WLR 1123, HL.

[30] *Ninemia* [1983] 1 WLR 1412, CA; *Garden Cottage Foods Ltd* v. *Milk Marketing Board* [1984] AC 130, HL; *Dellborg* v. *Corix*, 1980 CAT 541; *Conti Commodity Services Ltd* v. *Athis Philalithis*, 1980 CAT 386.

[31] See, e.g., *Practice Note* [1904] WN 203.

[32] e.g., Order 43, r.2, provides that a court can order an account or inquiry at any stage in a cause or matter, on application by summons; the inquiry would be referred to a Master in the Chancery Division and the Queen's Bench Division, and to a judge in the Commercial Court.

damages, in which the circumstances will be considered and a figure estimated to take account of any damage shown.

The inquiry will only be granted if the plaintiff was not entitled to the injunction,[33] and the damage complained of is neither trivial nor remote and the claim has not been unduly delayed.[34]

In practice, very few inquiries as to damages result from *Marevas.* This may be because of the difficulty of proving damages, but it is more likely that a plaintiff's claim is either not challenged, or that the parties have agreed a settlement which obviates the need for an inquiry. Even when the matter goes to a full trial it is often not appropriate to have a separate inquiry as to damages resulting from the injunction.

The power nevertheless exists, and it may well be worth considering as an effective reaction to an injunction in more cases than it is at present used. It would complement a realistic claim for costs against the applicant whose order has been discharged.

Costs of an inquiry as to damages are generally reserved, even if costs are awarded to the defendant on discharge of the injunction, so that the result of the inquiry can be seen before costs are awarded.

[33] *Griffith* v. *Blake* (1884) 27 Ch D 474; Order 29, r.1, and notes thereto.
[34] *Smith* v. *Day* (1882) 21 Ch D 421.

Limitations

CHAPTER 6

The position of banks and other third parties *(The consequences of a Mareva)*

The effect of a "Mareva"

In *Z Ltd* v. *A-Z and AA-LL* Lord Denning MR said[1] that: "a *Mareva* injunction is a method of attaching the asset itself. It operates *in rem* just as the arrest of a ship does."

Lest this should be misunderstood, Lord Denning later said[2] that: "It enables the seizure of assets so as to preserve them for the benefit of the creditor; but not to give a charge in favour of any particular creditor."

This latter qualification is vital to the effect of a *Mareva* injunction. It operates against the assets of the defendant, and so can be said to be *in rem*, but it does not create rights *in rem*. It does not of itself create any priority, lien, charge or security in those assets in favour of the party who made the *Mareva* application, nor in favour of any other party.[3] It is above all a remedy *in personam*, and breach of it makes the party responsible in contempt of court.

Thus, several points are noteworthy. First, a plaintiff with a judgment against the defendant can enforce it against his assets, whether covered by the *Mareva* or not, but only subject to the rights other persons have in the property in question. Secondly, during the currency of the *Mareva* any person with a claim against the defendant can proceed to judgment and enforce it. Thirdly, pre-existing liabilities to third parties will, especially in the case of banks, be respected even if not legally enforceable, and

[1] [1982] 1 QB 558, CA, at p. 573, A.   [2] At p. 573, C.
[3] *Pivaroff* v. *Chernabaeff* (1978) 16 SASR 329, when the *Mareva* was described as an undesirable species of anticipatory execution, at p. 334, by Bray CJ, must with respect have been based on a misunderstanding of the English *Mareva* cases. A *Mareva* cannot be registered as a land charge unless granted in aid of execution—*Stockler* v. *Fourways Estates Ltd.* [1984] 1 WLR 25, QBD, Kilner Brown J.

finally, third party bona fide purchasers for value without notice of the injunction will get good title regardless of the defendant's legal disability with respect to the assets.

Two cases are signally useful in this context. In *Cretanor Maritime Co Ltd* v. *Irish Marine Management Ltd*[4] the Irish charterers of a vessel executed a debenture, in 1975, in favour of an Irish bank, which resulted in a floating charge on all money due to them. The bank had the right to appoint a receiver to enforce the debenture, and a guarantee was given to it by a third party in case the charterers did not pay. In September 1976 the bank sought and obtained payment of the loan by the guarantor, and on assignment of the debenture he appointed a receiver.

In the meantime, disputes had arisen under the charterparty between the vessel's owners and the charterers, and a *Mareva* was granted against the charterer's funds until after an arbitration award was made. Although a compromise was reached it was not completed, and the owners proceeded to judgment. Unfortunately, there was insufficient money and the owners and the receiver were in competition to take the defendant's assets, such as they were, in partial satisfaction of their respective debts.

Donaldson J discharged the injunction and ordered that the defendant's certificate of deposit of funds be released to the receiver. The owners appealed, but it was held that they had no rights in the money itself, but only a right to prevent the defendant dealing with it so as to frustrate a judgment debt. Consequently, the rights of the debenture holder being created when the debenture itself was created were effective before the injunction, and meant that the funds were subject to the charge of the debenture holder, even though the receiver had not been appointed until after the injunction was granted. Buckley L J stated[5]:

> It seems to me . . . that it is not the case that any rights in the nature of a lien arise when a *Mareva* injunction is made. Under such an injunction the plaintiff has no rights against the assets. He may later acquire such rights if he obtains

[4] [1978] 1 WLR 966, CA.
[5] At p. 977, B.

judgment and can thereafter successfully levy execution upon them, but until that event his only rights are against the defendant personally.

Later, Buckley L J continued[6]:

> Taking into account the facts that the debenture holder is now an equitable assignee of the deposited fund, that the injunction gives the owners no present rights against the deposited fund but was made merely with a view to the retention of that fund in England so as to be available in the event of the owners' becoming able to levy execution upon it, and that, if the owners were hereafter to attempt to levy execution upon it, their rights as execution creditors would have to give way to prior rights in the fund, including the rights of the debenture holder, I think that the deposit certificate should be released to the receiver free from the injunction . . .

It is therefore the clear case that a *Mareva* simply preserves funds and assets, and does not give any rights over them which do not otherwise exist. Thus, if assets are subject to a trust or other equitable interest, or are later found to be the property of the plaintiff or another person, the *Mareva* can only assist in the court's relief. It cannot itself create an interest. What, therefore, is the answer for third parties with claims against the defendant? Must they, in the absence of priority to the plaintiff, proceed to judgment?

In *Iraqi Ministry of Defence* v. *Arcepey Shipping Co SA*[7] the position of third parties with outstanding debts due from the defendant was considered, and the judgment was straightforward in its rejection of the proposition that the defendant's creditors would have to proceed to judgment as the only way to get satisfaction for their claims. This is reasonable not only because the creditors would be put to expense, but also because the defendant would have his commercial reputation and standing reduced by having a judgment debt recorded against him, when the reason for not paying voluntarily was the imposition of a *Mareva* on

---

[6] At p. 979, A–B.
[7] *The Angel Bell, Gillespie Bros & Co Ltd intervening* [1980] 1 Lloyd's Rep. 632, QBD Comm Ct, Goff J; see Chapter 5.

the plaintiff's application. Thus, as was discussed in Chapter 5, third parties or defendants can apply to pay bona fide debts incurred in the ordinary course of business. If permission is not forthcoming from the court the creditor can only proceed to judgment, if his claim warrants it, and hope to beat the plaintiff's expected judgment and execution. If there are limited funds or assets available it will be a question of who can execute against them first, and the existence of a *Mareva* neither guarantees assets will remain at the time of judgment and execution, nor prevents others taking action themselves, or being allowed a variation to enable payments. There can be no special fund ordered for a plaintiff which he cannot obtain in any other way, or else the result would be the serious distortion of the law of insolvency.[8]

It may be objected that one order of the court, the *Mareva*, is negated by another order, the third party judgment. It must, however, be the case that as the *Mareva* is to prevent the defendant abusing the court's process and frustrating judgment, the judgment debt of a third party is as enforceable against the defendant's assets as the judgment of the plaintiff. Thus, a successful third party judgment creditor can apply for a garnishee order nisi against the defendant's debts, for example, money held for him by a bank. This creates a charge over the money, and when the order is made absolute the garnishee (the bank) is required to pay the money to the garnishor (the judgment creditor).[9] It may be wise for the garnishee to seek approval from the court, but in the absence of such an application he is in contempt of court if he does not obey the garnishee order absolute, and he must therefore act quickly on receipt of the order nisi.[10]

---

[8] *Ibid*, p. 636; *K/S A/S Admiral Shipping* v. *Portlink Ferries Ltd* [1984] 2 Lloyd's Rep. 166, CA, where variation was allowed despite the result that no money was left for the plaintiff.

[9] Order 49, r.1, r.2—the application is made *ex parte* supported by affidavit; *Rogers* v. *Whitely* [1892] AC 118—prior claims will be taken into account on an application by the claimant; see also Order 50—charging orders; the Supreme Court Act 1981, ss.40, 40A—attachment of debts; a garnishee order will not be made absolute if the defendant is insolvent—*Rainbow* v. *Moorgate Properties Ltd* [1975] 1 WLR 788, CA.

[10] See Chapter 9 for contempt.

In the same way, a judgment creditor can levy execution on the defendant's property by, for example, a writ of *fieri facias*, and the defendant would be required to deliver up the property in partial or total satisfaction of the debt.[11] Further, the creditor can start bankruptcy proceedings against an individual or apply for a winding-up order against a corporation. There seems no reason at all for a *Mareva* to impede a third party judgment creditor.

The provision of security

A *Mareva* can be discharged by a payment into court or the provision of security by the defendant, as was discussed in Chapter 5. Although a plaintiff originally seeking a *Mareva* to protect his position has no rights in the assets covered by the order, the provision of security or a payment into court promotes the plaintiff to the position of a secured creditor, and thus he is in a more favourable position than other, unsecured, creditors. This type of preference is not unusual because, for example, Order 14 applications for summary judgment are often set aside with leave to defend conditional on a payment in or the provision of security. The *Mareva* may, in practical terms, force the defendant to take action which favours the plaintiff, but this can hardly be a sustainable objection in the light of current practice. In any event, the defendant will normally be free to provide a bond or guarantee that the plaintiff's judgment debts will be met, which is a device equally favourable to the plaintiff without creating security in his favour, although the guarantor or provider of the bond may himself take security from the defendant.

Banks and their response to a "Mareva"

A banker's primary duty is to his customer, and no third party can interfere with the customer's account unless by

---

[11] This writ creates a charge over the goods—Sale of Goods Act 1893, s.26.

order of the court. In such a case the banker's contract with
his customer is suspended while the order is in force, and
the banker's primary duty is to the court.[12] (While the bank
is not ordinarily bound to pay any attention to the allegations of a third party, it may feel it ought to pay attention
to allegations of a trust or some similar warning, so that it
at least takes a decision whether to inquire into the circumstances or not.)

If banks are owed money by a customer whose account is
frozen they, in common with other creditors, may apply to
the court for a variation or discharge of the injunction, if
there has been no set-off clause included, and this has been
considered in Chapter 5. Any breach of the *Mareva* is of
course a contempt of court, and this aspect will be dealt with
in Chapter 9. The position of secured and other creditors
has already been discussed above as to the status of the
assets, and it is appropriate now to assess the liability of the
bank to its customer in the way it responds to the *Mareva*
injunction.

Once the order has been notified to the bank it is under a
duty not to deal with the defendant's assets. Thus, apart
from cheques backed by a cheque-card and other guaranteed
debits such as irrevocable documentary credits, the bank
must dishonour cheques and other negotiable instruments
presented for payment after notice of the order, regardless
of when these were drawn. The order of the court provides
a good defence to any action against the bank for breach of
contract.[13]

Although there is little authority on this point, it must
be crucial to the bank's responsibility to its customer to consider how these instruments are dishonoured.

If a bank returns cheques presented to it with the words
"injunction granted", or similar phrases, the holder of the
cheque knows that payment is not forthcoming because of

[12] *Tassell* v. *Cooper* (1850) 9 CB 509.
[13] *Denny, Mott & Dickson Ltd* v. *James B Fraser & Co Ltd* [1944] AC 265,
HL, Lord Macmillan at p. 272: "It is plain that a contract to do what it has
become illegal to do cannot be legally enforceable"; also, it can be said that
the customer's instructions are revoked, as in garnishee proceedings—
Rekstin v. *Severo Sibirsko Gosudustvemnoe AOK* [1933] 1 KB 47.

an order of the court. It would be better for a bank to say, if it be the case, that "funds sufficient but injunction granted against the account", or to use some similar phrase, so that the holder is left in no doubt that the reason for the dishonour is the granting of a prohibitory order.[14] Some statement should be made on the cheque because the London Clearing House requires all dishonoured cheques to carry written reasons for their return.

The bank may otherwise be in a weak position as against its customer if it simply dishonours the cheque by stating "insufficient funds", or "orders not to pay", or even "refer to drawer", because its action may be treated as analogous to a wrongful dishonour. The implication is thus not the account is the subject of a court order but that the customer cannot pay because he has no money, or is unwilling to pay, and is therefore the sort of person who gives cheques without being in funds or having arrangements to meet them; in short a person not to be trusted.

If the bank made a straightforward mistake when dishonouring a cheque an action for breach of contract and/or libel would be an option for the account holder to choose, and there seems no reason why the same course would not be open if a bank misdescribes the reasons for not honouring a cheque on a frozen account. It is not a question of suing a bank for abiding by a court order, but rather the taking of action to remedy or compensate for a misdescription.

Naturally, the customer ought first to ask his bank to alleviate the situation by sending correct information to the holders of returned cheques. Most banks will be able to do so because records are kept of returns and how they were presented, and this action is for the bank to take to protect its own position. Consequently, neither the plaintiff nor the defendant should have to pay for the costs involved.

[14] The holder then has a choice of waiting until the account is clear, or proceeding to judgment by suing on the debt and executing against the funds. It is doubtful whether he could sue on the dishonoured cheque because the dishonour is due to the court order; the underlying contract and its resultant obligation to pay is unaffected by the order.

Alternatively, the account holder can sue either for breach of contract or for libel. When he is not in trade an action for breach of contract is likely to result only in nominal damages, unless special damage can be proved.[15] Where he is a professional it could be argued that the same considerations as apply to traders would now cover him,[16] so that damage reasonably flowing from the breach would be awarded. On the other hand, an action for libel is more straightforward and, on the authorities, more likely to succeed.[17] Consequently, a defendant who finds his reputation damaged by a bank's incorrect statement on dishonoured cheques should seriously think of legal action, and banks must consider carefully how they deal with the return of unpaid paper when *Marevas* are involved. Although most of the clearing banks take care to advise holders of cheques precisely why they have been returned unpaid, there is no universal wording in constant use for injunctions, and so the likelihood of some misdescription is real.

The effect of a "Mareva" on Legal Aid

The Legal Aid Act 1974[18] provides for assessment of persons for legal aid. Although a *Mareva* does not create rights in the assets frozen, it may affect the value of them, and therefore the assessment officer can take the reduced open market value of the asset into account. Further, he can use his discretion to allow for contingent liabilities or to take into account the general circumstances of the case, so that a *Mareva* may well affect a party's entitlement to legal aid in some instances.

---

[15] *Gibbons* v. *Westminster Bank Ltd* [1939] 2 KB 882.

[16] As to traders (including merchants, commercial agents and brokers) see *Robin* v. *Steward* (1854) 14 CB 595; *Wilson* v. *United Counties Bank Ltd* [1920] AC 102 (especially pp. 112–13).

[17] *Jayson* v. *Midland Bank Ltd* [1968] 1 Lloyd's Rep. 409, CA; *Davidson* v. *Barclays Bank Ltd.* (1940) 56 TLR 343 (especially Hilbery J at p. 349); *Baker* v. *Australia & New Zealand Bank Ltd* [1958] NZLR 907, Shorland J; *Pyke* v. *Hibernian Bank Ltd* [1950] IR 195.

[18] Section 11; see also Legal Aid (Assessment of Resources) Regulations 1980, Sched. 3, Rules for Computing Disposable Capital, rules 2, 12, and 14.

CHAPTER 7

The "Mareva" and fraudulent or criminal activity

The *Mareva* injunction has an important role to play in combating fraud and crime. When it is used in relation to fraud by private plaintiffs its scope is clear; the same principles apply as on any other claim, whether in contract or otherwise, and only the field of use changes. Sought by the police, though, against the dissipation of assets held by persons charged with criminal offences, its role moves out of the private field and into the public area of criminal law, overshadowed by the responsibility of the police and government. Use of any power, statutory or otherwise, against an unconvicted person, however strong the evidence appears, is contentious. Anything which touches upon the liberty of the individual becomes of greater importance than the immediate facts, and thus the application of a civil injunction against a person charged with a criminal offence, precisely because he has been so charged, is a departure of note from the usual *Mareva* practice.

In fact, it is a potentially powerful departure, and the inherent jurisdiction of the court to decide the justice and convenience of an order must, subject to the guidelines of the courts and statutory enactments, it is submitted, be left unfettered. The complexity of modern crime and the rewards to be gained merit a flexible approach to the proceeds of such crimes, and the assets of the criminals involved.

Further, the *Mareva* can be of use in non-commercial crime to preserve funds pending a civil claim for assault, for example, but this extension will have to depend on the victims deciding that it is worthwhile to take civil action.

Part of the problem of commercial crime, however, is the reluctance of the parties to involve the police. This need not stop a plaintiff taking action in contract or tort, or under some other category, and using a *Mareva* injunction in the usual way, and such a move is particularly helpful in the resolution of disputes involving bills of exchange and documentary credits, because of the absolute nature of the obligation to pay.

"Marevas" and documentary credits and bills of exchange

The autonomy of documentary credits and bills of exchange is now a clear part of English law. So far as bills of exchange are concerned, the cases of *Montecchi* v. *Shimco (UK) Ltd*,[1] and *Navone* v. *Shimco (UK) Ltd*[1a] confirmed that a *Mareva* injunction can be granted against the holder of a bill so that the proceeds of it are frozen. For example, on payment by the acceptor the holder (payee) is ordered not to dispose of the funds pending an action against him on the underlying contract. It should be noted that this does not interfere with the Order 14 procedure for summary judgment when suing on a bill of exchange that has been dishonoured, but it does prevent the successful Order 14 plaintiff making himself proof against a favourable judgment on the defendant's counterclaim. It follows, therefore, that the defendant who is unable to rely on the accepted defences to Order 14 proceedings on a bill, that is illegality, fraud, total failure of consideration, or partial failure of a liquidated sum, can nevertheless preserve the funds in question by applying for a *Mareva*. This is possible whether the dispute is simply contractual, or when there are elements of fraud, but because the applicant will have to show a good arguable counterclaim, together with satisfactory evidence of risk that the plaintiff will make himself judgment-proof, the existence of fraud in the underlying contract can only be of help so far as the latter allegation is concerned. It must also be considered that the courts will be more willing to grant a *Mareva* where fraud is shown, even though the fraud is insufficient to found an immediate defence on the Order 14 claim.

[1] [1979] 1 WLR 1180, CA.
[1a] [1979] 1 WLR 1180, CA.

The use of bills of exchange in world-wide commerce, although on the decrease, means that the fact a holder is resident abroad is of little note in these *Mareva* proceedings, as it is only one element in the pattern which has to be considered. However, the fact that the plaintiff against whom a *Mareva* was sought was based abroad was relevant in the *Montecchi* case, because of the possibility of enforcement of an English judgment, even if he intended to remove the funds. As Bridge L J said[2]:

> Here, for all we know, the two Italian plaintiffs, the sellers of the goods in respect of which the bills of exchange were given, are persons of perfectly sound financial standing in Italy. The actions have been brought in this country on the bills of exchange. The defendant company have had the advantage of being able to make their counterclaim in each case for the damages that they say are due to them in respect of defects in the goods. If those counterclaims are eventually successful, then they will result in judgments in this country which will be enforceable in Italy under the procedure provided by the Foreign Judgments (Reciprocal Enforcement) Act 1933 and orders made thereunder.

The same considerations must now apply to persons based in a Convention country under the 1968 Brussels Convention, when this is brought into force by the Civil Jurisdiction and Judgments Act 1982.

Applying the *Mareva* principles consistently, therefore, fear that an automatic grant of a *Mareva* would have the effect of destroying the bill of exchange as the equivalent of cash is reduced because of the need for the defendant to raise both an arguable counterclaim and show some risk. Given that double hurdle, it is likely that an Order 14 defendant on a bill of exchange would be able to apply successfully for a *Mareva* in only a few, justified, cases.

The position with regard to documentary credits is more complicated. The obligation of the buyer to pay is transferred to the bank, and the requirement that a confirmed documentary credit, almost always irrevocable, must be

[2] *Ibid*, at p. 1184.

honoured on presentation of the correct documents, is fundamental, and the buyer cannot order the bank not to pay the seller/beneficiary.[3] This is because the opening of the confirmed credit constitutes a real bargain between the bank and the seller which gives the seller/beneficiary the right to sue for the performance of the bank's absolute obligation.

If, however, there is clear evidence of fraud, the court will interfere with the usual commercial practice, and grant an injunction to prevent the bank paying,[4] but not if there are mere allegations of some fraudulent activity.[5] This is not a *Mareva* injunction, but one designed to overshadow the bank's obligation to pay according to the terms of the credit because of the evidence of fraud. For example, the wrongful but skilful backdating of a bill of lading is likely to mean that the bank has to pay on presentation of the documents because of the doctrine of strict compliance. The bank is bound to look at the documents as documents, and not to look behind them. Thus, despite any objection from the customer, the beneficiary is entitled to be paid, because the documents appear correct. However, backdating of a document in such circumstances is forgery,[6] and this might give a basis to an injunction against the bank if it can be shown that the seller/beneficiary had knowledge of the fraud. The courts' approach to this problem was explained by Sir John Donaldson MR in *Bollvinter Oil SA* v. *Chase Manhattan Bank*[7]:

> Before leaving this appeal, we should like to add a word about the circumstances in which an *ex parte* injunction should be issued which prohibits a bank from paying under an irrevocable letter of credit or a purchase bond or guarantee. The

[3] *Stein* v. *Hambros Bank* (1921) 9 Ll. L. Rep. 433; *Hamzeh Malas & Sons* v. *British Imex Industries Ltd* [1958] 2 QB 127, CA—injunction against bank refused; *Soc Metallurgique d'Aubrives et Villerupt* v. *British Bank for Foreign Trade* (1922) 11 Ll. L. Rep. 168—order by the buyer not to pay not upheld.
[4] *Elian and another* v. *Matsas and others* [1966] 2 Lloyd's Rep. 495, CA; *United City Merchants Ltd* v. *Royal Bank of Canada* [1982] 2 Lloyd's Rep 1, HL.
[5] *Discount Records Ltd* v. *Barclays Bank Ltd* [1975] 1 WLR 315.
[6] Forgery and Counterfeiting Act 1981; see s.9(1)(*g*).
[7] [1984] 1 WLR 392, CA, at p. 393.

unique value of such a letter, bond or guarantee is that the beneficiary can be completely satisfied that whatever disputes may thereafter arise between him and the bank's customer in relation to the performance or indeed existence of the underlying contract, the bank is personally undertaking to pay him provided that the specified conditions are met. In requesting his bank to issue such a letter, bond or guarantee, the customer is seeking to take advantage of this unique characteristic. If, save in the most exceptional cases, he is to be allowed to derogate from the bank's personal and irrevocable undertaking, given be it again noted at his request, by obtaining an injunction restraining the bank from honouring that undertaking, he will undermine what is the bank's greatest asset, however large and rich it may be, namely its reputation for financial and contractual probity. Furthermore, if this happens at all frequently, the value of all irrevocable letters of credit and performance bonds and guarantees will be undermined.

Judges who are asked, often at short notice and *ex parte*, to issue an injunction restraining payment by a bank under an irrevocable letter of credit or performance bond or guarantee should ask whether there is any challenge to the validity of the letter, bond or guarantee itself. If there is not or if the challenge is not substantial, *prima facie* no injunction should be granted and the bank should be left free to honour its contractual obligation, although restrictions may well be imposed upon the freedom of the beneficiary to deal with the money after he has received it. The wholly exceptional case where an injunction may be granted is where it is proved that the bank knows that any demand for payment already made or which may thereafter be made will clearly be fraudulent. But the evidence must be clear, both as to the fact of fraud and as to the bank's knowledge. It would certainly not normally be sufficient that this rests upon the uncorroborated statement of the customer, for irreparable damage can be done to a bank's credit in the relatively brief time which must elapse between the granting of such an injunction and an application by the bank to have it discharged. The appeal will be dismissed.

The above guidelines indicate the continuing difficulty of obtaining an injunction against the bank. Can a *Mareva* injunction nevertheless be granted to restrain the defendant (not the bank) from dealing with the funds, once the credit has been paid? Apart from the view that no *Mareva* will be granted if the effect would be to prevent a bank dealing with the proceeds of a documentary credit for the benefit of a beneficiary abroad,[8] there seems no reason at all why, given the double test necessary for a *Mareva*, the buyer could not get an order restraining the seller/beneficiary from disposing of the funds received under the arrangements pending an action on the underlying contract. This would again apply whether there was an allegation of fraud, or a more basic contractual disagreement. In an appropriate case, the order could cover the general funds and assets of the seller, as well as the credit proceeds.

Such an order cannot affect the day-to-day operation of the documentary credit system, nor does it involve a change in the relevant law and practice. However, there may be a difficulty in logistical terms if a bank, on whom a *Mareva* is served, freezes the bank accounts of a customer, but is unaware of whether he has any independent arrangement with them whereby he is the beneficiary under a documentary credit.[9] This could be a particular problem if the credit was transferable, as the bank records might not make it clear to the staff dealing with the transaction who was the real beneficiary, and whether the funds were properly within an order, assuming that they were actually aware of the injunction.

If the *Mareva* is wide enough it will catch future receipts as well as present funds, but what if the money from the credit is not paid into an account or, as still occurs, the beneficiary has a right to have a bill of exchange accepted by the bank, rather than receiving the money by immediate transfer? Clearly, it remains the beneficiary's money, and he is in breach of the order if he deals with, or if he purports to assign the benefit of, it, but is the bank in breach for allowing him to receive it? The answer must depend on whether the branch involved has been served with the order, or has otherwise learnt of it, and whether the terms

---

[8] *The Bhoja Trader* [1981] 2 Lloyd's Rep. 258.
[9] Referred to by Kerr L J in *Z Ltd* v. *A-Z and AA-LL* [1982] 1 QB 588, CA, at p. 591, E.

of the order are wide enough to include these proceeds. Despite the expense, which the plaintiff will have to pay, it would be logical and wise for a bank to issue directions to its relevant branches to forestall the dissipation of such funds, for any alternative would be to give a seller/beneficiary a valuable loophole and a convenient escape route. Much therefore depends on an appropriate wording of the original order, and notice to the bank that receipt of funds under a documentary credit arrangement is suspected or known.

Further remedies

The usual contractual remedies apply on a breach of the underlying contract connected with a documentary credit or a bill of exchange, but there may also be tortious conduct in the issue of false documents and representations, and this avenue of claim can be taken when no immediate or satisfactory contractual relationship exists. For example, if a false certificate of quality is issued, but no responsibility attaches to the seller, and no clear fraud sufficient to obtain an injunction against the paying bank exists, there might also be difficulty in seeking a *Mareva* against the seller because of the lack of an arguable case against him, as well as the need for evidence of risk. Why should the party issuing the false certificate not be sued? There would be a *prima facie* action for deceit,[10] even if the false certificate could have been checked and verified,[11] and a *Mareva* would be possible against the assets of the certifying company or firm. Whether it would be worthwhile to take this action depends on the circumstances, as does the question of tracing the originator of a forged document, but it does provide an additional remedy, especially if all other claims fail.

---

[10] The defendant must know of or be reckless as to the false instrument:— *Derry* v. *Peek* (1889) 14 App. Cas. 337; see also *Bradford Building Society* v. *Borders* [1941] 2 All ER 2057, HL; *West London Commercial Bank* v. *Kitson* (1884) 13 QBD 360, CA.

[11] *Central Railway of Venezuela* v. *Kisch* (1867) LR 2 HL 199.

In appropriate fraud cases a plaintiff could sue for conspiracy,[12] although in international matters this is notoriously difficult to bring within the jurisdiction of the English courts, whether for civil or criminal purposes.[13] Certainly, some of the large multinational frauds are planned and executed in several countries, but if the main elements can be traced to England, and some, if not all of the damage occurs here, a *prima facie* case at least could be made out and a *Mareva* sought to freeze traceable assets pending further action.

Criminal offences and commerce

The opportunity to initiate criminal proceedings against wrong-doers in the commercial field is rarely taken. There are significant problems involved in jurisdiction of the criminal courts, and there is little incentive, financially, for the victims of commercial fraud to engage police interest in their misfortunes. The same need not be true of crimes of violence, where the advantage of reporting the matter to the police includes the right to apply to the Criminal Injuries Compensation Board for compensation.[14] Whether in commercial crime or generally, the criminal law does not give much assistance to parties seeking to preserve the assets of a defendant pending suit (although plans for reform are considered below). Nevertheless, it should be mentioned

---

[12] A modern invention in civil cases, according to *Midland Bank Trust Co Ltd* v. *Green (No. 3)* [1982] Ch. 529; see *Crofter Hand-Woven Harris Tweed Co Ltd* v. *Veitch* [1942] AC 435; *Lonrho Ltd* v. *Shell Petroleum Co Ltd (No. 2)* [1982] AC 173; the case of *Z Ltd* v. *A-Z and AA-LL* [1982] 1 QB 558, CA was based on a fraud of £2 million.

[13] *Attorney-General's Reference (No 1 of 1982)* [1983] QB 751, CA; *R* v. *Doot* [1973] AC 807; *R* v. *Scott* [1975] AC 819; *Board of Trade* v. *Owen* [1957] AC 602.

[14] Criminal Injuries Compensation Scheme 1964 (revised 1979). See the 19th Report of the Board for a general description of its activities, 1983 HMSO (Cmnd 9093). There now has to be an injury giving rise to a claim of at least £400 before compensation is payable. Suing for trespass or assault could be worthwhile; see *White* v. *Commissioner of Metropolitan Police, The Times*, 24 April 1982, but few civil actions in fact take place. Note the bar against civil action when summary proceedings have been started under the Offences against the Person Act 1861 (ss.42–45).

that many instances of commercial fraud will include
elements of theft,[15] forgery and counterfeiting,[16] and conspiracy.[17] It remains to be seen though whether much use
will be made of those powers contained in the criminal law,
despite an increasing awareness of the need to bring official
nationwide and international organizations into the resolution of large-scale fraud.[18] One advantage of the criminal
aspect of fraud is the possibility of the police seeking orders
against defendants, rather than relying on the individual
victim to act, and this is considered below.

Public policy

Two recent cases, *R* v. *Thompson (Michael)*[19] and *R* v.
Thomas (Keith)[20] are indicative of the views of the Criminal
Court of Appeal. In *Thompson* the defendant was a computer operator who had been employed in a Kuwaiti bank
in Kuwait. During his work there he had opened five bank
accounts in his name, and programmed the bank computer
to credit them with customers' money. After he returned to
England he opened bank accounts here, and then wrote to
the Kuwaiti bank asking for certain funds to be telexed to
his English accounts. When the fraud was discovered he was
charged with obtaining property by deception. He submitted
that the English court had no jurisdiction because the property had been obtained in Kuwait, but he was nonetheless
convicted, and the conviction was upheld. Clearly, it was
said, the request for the transfer by telex had been made in

[15] See Theft Act 1968, s.15 and generally.
[16] See Forgery and Counterfeiting Act 1981, especially s.1 which includes
the making of a false instrument with the intention of inducing someone
to accept it as genuine, and consequently to act to his, or another person's,
detriment.
[17] Now reduced, for criminal purposes, by the Criminal Law Act 1977.
Conspiracy to commit a substantial criminal offence, and to defraud,
remain as indictable offences; see above fns. 12 and 13 for further discussion
on conspiracy.
[18] The work of the International Maritime Bureau, part of the ICC, is
noteworthy in this respect.
[19] [1984] 1 WLR 962, CA.
[20] [1984] 3 WLR 321, CA.

England, and this was a false representation that the balances were genuine. Consequently, the money had been obtained by deception.

This was a robust and practical interpretation of the law, avoiding undue technicality and restriction, and serves to reinforce the general public policy that fraudulent activity should not be allowed to flourish. In the circumstances, it must be the case that the Kuwaiti bank could have applied for and obtained a *Mareva* injunction, preventing the disposal of the funds pending civil litigation against the defendant, whether this was with a view to civil compensation alone, or with an application by the Crown for a compensation order at the criminal trial. The bank would have had the necessary *locus standi* because it would have a legal right to sue for the recovery of the money.[21]

In *Thomas* the defendant was working in Italy, and fraudulently transferred funds from his employer's bank account to a false one in England. He had been convicted in his absence by the Italian courts, and sentenced to imprisonment and a fine. In England he was charged with theft of the money, and submitted that he should not be tried here because he had already been convicted in Italy. Despite this defence he was convicted, and appealed, but this was dismissed on the basis that although he had been prosecuted for the same offence, such a plea in bar was not applicable when he had not appeared before the foreign court, and was in no real danger because of his foreign conviction. The Court of Appeal emphasized that it would be unjust and offend public confidence if the defendant had been allowed to escape prosecution[22]:

> In our judgment, public confidence would be offended were the prosecution . . . to have been stopped because of the conviction recorded in the accused's absence in the circumstances of this case, and an injustice would have been done if this trial had not taken place. . .

---

[21] Both in tort and in contract, especially as the transfer of the money was wrong by Kuwaiti and English law and in breach of the defendant's contract of employment; see fn. 23, below.

[22] [1984] 3 WLR 321, at p. 326.

If he were not convicted and punished here he would walk free and suffer not at all for his theft of the sum of £95,721 3p from his employers.

Here, too, the employer could have obtained a *Mareva* injunction pending a civil action, or the outcome of the criminal trial, as his right to return of the money, or damages, would be sufficient to give him a legal interest.[23] In all such cases a civil action could utilize a conviction in the criminal courts, because of the heavy burden on the prosecution to prove its case, compared to the comparatively easier burden of a plaintiff in civil matters where the balance of probabilities is the yardstick. Indeed, because of the prosecution's heavy burden, it may be said that an acquittal in the criminal courts is no insurmountable hurdle to success in a civil claim.

"Marevas" and the police

The attitude of the Criminal Court of Appeal in *Thompson* and *Thomas* above has been reflected in recent civil cases where the police have applied for *Mareva* injunctions against suspected criminals.

In *Chief Constable of Kent* v. *V and another*[24] the defendant had been arrested and charged with forgery and theft of over £16,000. The money was believed by the police to be in his bank accounts, and to prevent it being dissipated pending trial the Chief Constable applied *ex parte* to Skinner J for an injunction in *Mareva* terms.[25] This was granted, but Beldam J, on the hearing of the originating summons, only continued the order until the Court of Appeal could hear the matter. By a majority, the court considered that an injunction was right and just, although

[23] See fn. 21 above, and discussion earlier at p. 30.
[24] [1983] 1 QB 34, CA, Lord Denning MR, Donaldson and Slade L JJ. Slade L J dissented from the majority, even though he acknowledged the practical advantages of the order.
[25] Based on *West Mercia Constabulary* v. *Wagener and others* [1982] 1 WLR 127, where Forbes J had granted an injunction to prevent the defendant disposing of his assets pending trial of a mail-order fraud. The application then was based on Order 29, r.2(1).

there were differing views from Lord Denning MR and Donaldson L J.

The main problem in all such cases is whether the Chief Constable or other head of the police unit has a legal right or interest sufficient to enable him to make an application.[26] Clearly, it could be argued that it was just for the proceeds of an alleged crime to be frozen pending the trial, but was it a permissible extension of the *Mareva*?

The "good arguable case" hurdle in a purely civil *Mareva* would have to be replaced in practice by the need to show that the defendant had been, or was about to be, charged with an indictable offence connected with the assets to be injuncted. The same test of risk as to dissipation would apply without modification, although the fact of a charge itself might reduce the need for further evidence.

The benefit of a *Mareva* in such cases is more valid if the origination of the funds is considered. The *Mareva* in ordinary civil cases does not depend on the subject-matter of the injunction having any connection with the defendant other than being owned by him. This is consistent with the fact that a *Mareva* creates no proprietary interest[27] in the assets, but merely preserves them pending a favourable judgment and execution. The *Mareva* in criminal cases would rely on the wrongful possession of the funds or assets on the basis that they had been obtained by crime. Thus, possession of them would in itself be wrong, whereas possession of assets in ordinary civil claims is rarely improper unless some proprietary interest on the plaintiff's part is alleged.

In fact, Lord Denning MR saw no problem in the Chief Constable's position. The objections raised against the *West Mercia Constabulary*[28] case were dismissed on the grounds that the addition of "final" to "interlocutory" in section 37(1)

---

[26] See Order 29, r.1 p. 33, and *The Siskina* discussion, p. 30.
[27] See p. 61.
[28] See fn. 25 above; also *North London Railway Co* v. *Great Northern Railway Co* (1883) 11 QBD 30; *Gouriet* v. *Union of Post Office Workers* [1978] AC 435, HL, especially at p. 501 and 516; *The Siskina* [1979] AC 210, HL, at p. 256.

of the Supreme Court Act 1981[29] "confers a new and exten-
sive jurisdiction on the High Court to grant an injunction".[30]
Thus, because the police have a duty to enforce the law, and
to do their best to recover stolen goods and catch criminals,
they have a sufficient interest to apply for an injunction.

Donaldson L J, as he then was, agreed with the order, but
only in so far as it related to money traceable as coming
from the victims of the fraud.[31] However, he felt that a legal
or equitable right was necessary, but this could be based on
the right common law "can and should" give the police to
freeze money in a bank account if it can be shown to have
been obtained from another party as a result of crime.[32] This
right has the added advantage that it can be exercised on
behalf of victims of crime where the individual amounts lost
would not justify civil action, as well as those cases where
the victim might contemplate his own claim. In either
case, of course, the Chief Constable sues in his public role,
and not to recover anything for the police. His right to sue
is an extension of his duty to uphold the law, although Slade
L J considered this extension of police powers was raising
too many incidental questions.

It is interesting to note that Donaldson L J required the
police to issue a writ claiming at least a declaration that
the Chief Constable was entitled to retain the money, but
Lord Denning MR considered that no writ was necessary.
The difference in approach reflects the different bases on
which the right to sue and claim was fixed.

The above cases were followed by *Chief Constable of
Hampshire* v. *A Ltd and others*.[33] The police had charged
the directors of two garage companies with conspiracy to

[29] See p. 10.
[30] [1983] 1 QB 34, at p. 42.
[31] *Malone* v. *Metropolitan Police Commissioner* [1980] QB 49, where the
police were ordered to return property seized, was distinguished on the
grounds that an order could not be made against property which was
clearly the defendant's, and not stolen or the proceeds of crime. If the police
have a legal interest to enable them to apply for an injunction, should the
origination of the money or assets matter, as it does not in civil cases?
[32] Based partially on the common law right of seizure in *Chic Fashions
(West Wales) Ltd* v. *Jones* [1968] 2 QB 299.
[33] (1984) 79 Cr App R 30, CA.

defraud customers and finance houses by issuing financial documents with a falsely high sale price, and selling cars with false milometers. The mortgages on the garages had been paid off by the proceeds of these activities, and the properties had then been sold. Some £177,000 of the sale money was traced, either held at the bank or by the parties' solicitors. The Chief Constable therefore applied by originating summons for a *Mareva* injunction against the defendants, but this was refused. On appeal, it was held that while the type of order sought was permissible and could be granted, this was not an appropriate case to do so because the money had not been identified as the profits from crime. Therefore, while the right of the police was essentially confirmed, the need to show that the assets are the proceeds of crime does narrow, albeit slightly, the scope of the new-found extension of the *Mareva*.

The *Mareva* in criminal matters is a valid order. The only practical reservation must be that proceedings for contempt are more of a threat to banks and other independent parties than to those already charged with serious criminal offences. It may thus be considered that conditions as to bail for a defendant can be combined in practice with the *Mareva* injunction to create an effective bar against dissipation. What, however, would happen if the defendant were acquitted? Could it then be said that damages for having imposed an injunction would be ordered against the police? The simplest answer is to apply the same rules as on arrest, so that if the application is made reasonably, based on reliable evidence and suspicion, the police should not have to be penalized in damages. Alternatively, an inquiry as to damages could be ordered in the usual way.

The Hodgson Committee Report

In the circumstances outlined above, it is instructive to consider the recommendations of a report initiated by the Howard League[34] on the present state of the law relating

[34] Sir Derek Hodgson (chairman), *Profits of Crime and their Recovery* (London: Heinemann).

to forfeiture, compensation and restitution of property in criminal proceedings, and criminal bankruptcy. The report was based on private research, but the work had the co-operation of the Home Office, whose general responsibility covers the administration of the criminal justice system.

The impetus for the report was the decision of the House of Lords in *R* v. *Cuthbertson*,[35] following the "Operation Julie" drugs trial at the Bristol Crown Court. The judge made an order for the forfeiture of the assets of the defendants, on conviction, under section 27(1) of the Misuse of Drugs Act 1971, in view of the vast sums of money made by them out of the purchase and sale of illegal drugs. In fact, most of the money appeared to be abroad, but some £750,000 was traced in England and overseas. On appeal, the Court of Appeal upheld the order, but the House of Lords allowed a further appeal, although not without expressing some reluctance. It was held that the power of the criminal courts did not extend to money abroad, nor to all the profits associated with crime, and specifically, the court had no power to order confiscation of assets under section 27 if the defendants had been convicted of conspiracy.

This decision caused considerable disquiet, and illustrates the problem that the large sums of money amassed by criminals can easily outweigh the deterrence of conviction and sentence. Further, there was little scope for civil action by the victims of the criminals because of the difficulty of assessing who were the victims, and how they had suffered damages as a result of the activities of the accused.

The case combined with the general uncertainty as to the nature of criminal compensation and forfeiture, and the necessity to make better use of the powers of the criminal courts,[36] to provide a starting point for the Committee. One

---

[35] [1981] AC 470, HL (and *R* v. *Kemp* (1979) 69 Cr App R 330); see also *R* v. *Riley* (1984) 78 Cr App R 121, CA.

[36] The main powers of the criminal courts are to make a Criminal Bankruptcy Order, under ss.39–41, and Sched. 2 to the Powers of the Criminal Courts Act 1973, if no compensation has been awarded; see generally *DPP* v. *Anderson* [1978] 2 All ER 512, HL, and *R* v. *Downing* (1980) 71 Cr App R 316, CA, and to make a compensation order under ss. 35–38 of the same Act, see *R* v. *Inwood* (1975) 60 Cr App R 70, CA; *R* v. *Schofield* [1978] 2 All ER 705, CA; *R* v. *Daly* [1974] 1 WLR 133; both orders can only relate to offences for which the defendant has been convicted, or which have been taken into consideration. Note also s.67 of the Criminal Justice Act 1982, and the Forfeiture Act 1982, together with *In re Royse, decd.* [1984] 3 WLR 784, CA.

set of recommendations has direct relevance to the present discussion, and is entirely appropriate given the police powers to seek injunctions discussed above. The suggestion is that there should be a pre-trial restraint on the defendant, ordered by a High Court judge on an *ex parte* application, based on oral or affidavit evidence, when a *prima facie* case of an indictable offence has been made out, and there was a likelihood that a fine or compensation order of over £10,000 would be imposed on conviction. No risk of dissipation was suggested as a precondition to such an order being granted.

The defendant would have the usual right to apply for a variation or discharge, as would third parties adversely affected by the order, and the trial judge would have the power to award compensation or order an inquiry as to damages if the defendant was later acquitted.[37]

An additional recommendation was that a victim would be able to enter a caveat against discharge of the injunction, while pursuing a civil claim for damages. This removes the necessity for him to seek a separate injunction, as well as avoiding the costs of a duplication of proceedings. To assist in the new scheme, a receiver or custodian of injuncted property would be appointed to investigate the circumstances, as well as to hold and if necessary manage the assets of the defendant.

The implementation of these recommendations will, if approved by the government, place on a statutory basis what many hope is already at least a partial solution to the problem, based on the cases discussed above. Certainly, an objection could be raised that compensation for the acquitted defendant would be difficult to ascertain, but this is part of the problem of damages for a wrongful injunction generally.[38] Further, it might be suggested that a defendant would be at a disadvantage in paying for his defence if his assets are controlled and isolated in this way, but he can apply for a variation, and his assets remain his property until further order. It may, nevertheless, be necessary to

---

[37] Similar to Order 43, r.2, and see p. 82.
[38] See p. 59.

consider how Legal Aid might operate in such circumstances.[39] On balance, the Hodgson Report can be welcomed
as a logical development in the application of interlocutory
and final injunctions to protect the interests of innocent parties.[40]

[39] See discussion at p. 68; a defendant could apply for a variation to pay
his defence costs in the usual way, see Chapter 5.

[40] Other recommendations were that there should be no maximum on the
amount of a confiscation order, but that notice of the seeking of the order
should be given to the defendant to enable him to prepare his case. Also,
the restitution provisions of the Theft Act 1968, in s.28, should be repealed
as unnecessary, and that further thought should be given to the forfeiture
rules.

CHAPTER 8

Ancillary and connected orders of the court

This chapter seeks to outline the more common orders associated with *Marevas*, so that the overall jurisdiction of the court can be considered. A skilful choice of ancillary orders makes the *Mareva* an even more powerful weapon, and it must be noted that the grant of a *Mareva* does not preclude any other order from being used, whether discussed below or not.

The Anton Piller Order

In some cases it is vital for a plaintiff to ensure that evidence in the defendant's possession is not destroyed or disposed of so as to make it difficult, if not impossible, to prove his case. In these circumstances an application can be made *ex parte* for a mandatory injunction to allow the plaintiff's solicitor to inspect documents and chattels on the defendant's premises, and to take photographs or copies of them.[1] The order must be clear and concise, and based on full disclosure before the court. It is founded on the court's inherent jurisdiction to prevent a defendant frustrating judgment, in this case by destroying or disposing of either the evidence or the subject-matter of the dispute, before the proceedings have begun. It thus works hand in hand with the *Mareva* order under section 37 of the Supreme Court Act 1981,

---

[1] *EMI* v. *Pandit* [1975] 1 WLR 302; *Anton Piller KG* v. *Manufacturing Process Ltd* [1976] Ch 55; *Practice Note* [1982] 1 WLR 1420, CA; *Universal City Studios Inc.* v. *Hubbard* [1984] Ch 225, CA; *Digital Equipment Corp* v. *Darkcrest Ltd* [1984] Ch 512, Falconer J; Supreme Court Act 1981, ss.23 and 72; Appendix I; during proceedings Order 29, r.2—detention and preservation of subject-matter of cause or matter.

88   *The Mareva Injunction*

although the tests to be applied are stricter because it is a draconian power.[2]

The plaintiff must show first that he has a strong *prima facie* case; secondly, that the defendant has incriminating evidence in his possession which he is likely to dispose of before an *inter partes* hearing, and, thirdly, that he will suffer serious damage as a result. A list of the premises to be inspected should be placed in a schedule to the order.

The injunction often includes an order to give details on affidavit of assets and other premises, or to deliver up goods, and this fits neatly in with other orders ancillary to a *Mareva*, discussed below. The Anton Piller Order is most often encountered in the Chancery Division where injunctions are heard in open court, so that a request for the court to sit *in camera* is essential to minimize publicity and maintain complete surprise.[3]

The cases where these orders are essential are to do with copyright, patents, trademarks, passing off, industrial espionage and abuse of confidential information, although there is in practice no limitation on the type of action. The remedy sought and the reasons for it will determine whether an Anton Piller is granted or not.

The order is not a "civil" search warrant, and only recourse a plaintiff has if his solicitor, who as an officer of the court is entrusted with implementing the order, is refused entry is to seek to commit the defendant for contempt. Force cannot be used and, although the defendant risks being penalized for contempt, his desire to take legal advice before permitting entry has been recognized as reasonable.[4]

The order cannot be used to discover evidence on which to base a later claim,[5] but it can probably extend to overseas

[2] *Per* Donaldson J in *Yousif* v. *Salama* [1980] 1 WLR 1540, at p. 1544.
[3] E.g. *Vapormatic Co Ltd* v. *Sporex Ltd* [1976] 1 WLR 939; orders are granted elsewhere, e.g. in the Family Division—*Emanuel* v. *Emanuel* [1982] 1 WLR 669, Wood J.
[4] *Hallmark Cards Inc* v. *Image Arts Ltd* [1977] FSR 150.
[5] *Hytrac Conveyors Ltd* v. *Conveyors International Ltd* [1983] FSR 63, CA.

premises so long as the defendant is within the jurisidiction of the English courts.[6]

Anton Piller is potentially as far-reaching as the *Mareva* and involves many potential difficulties, not only because of its interference with the rights of individuals and companies, but also because of its other effects on third parties. In the context of the *Mareva* and this work, however, it can only be described as a formidable ally in preserving evidence and preventing empty judgments.

Delivery up of chattels

In some cases the usual *Mareva* order restraining the defendant from disposing of his assets within the jurisdiction is not effective enough to safeguard the plaintiff's position. In these circumstances an additional order can be made for delivery up of the defendant's chattels so that they are in the safe custody of someone who will not allow them to be dissipated, usually the plaintiff's solicitor or a receiver appointed by the High Court.[7]

Thus, such an order is restricted to cases where the contempt powers on breach of an injunction are thought not to be enough to deter the defendant. There must therefore be clear evidence that he will be likely to dispose of the chattels deliberately to deprive the plaintiff of a meaningful and effective judgment. There must also be evidence or an inference that the chattels are the defendant's as a result of some illegal acts, whether directly or because they have been bought with the proceeds.

The defendant can retain his clothes, and the tools of his trade (including motor-vehicles and, if appropriate, farm implements and livestock). Furnishings are also generally

---

[6] *Cook Industries Ltd* v. *Galliher* [1979] Ch 439, Templeman J—flat in Paris, order for inventory to be made; in *Protector Alarms Ltd* v. *Maxim Alarms Ltd* [1978] FSR 442, Goulding J refused an order concerning premises in Scotland on the grounds of internal comity within the United Kingdom. See also *Altertext Inc.* v. *Advanced Data Communications Ltd.* [1985] 1 WLR 457, Ch D, Scott J.

[7] *CBS United Kingdom Ltd* v. *Lambert and another* [1983] 1 Ch 37, CA; see Appendix I; note also Order 29, r.2—detention or preservation of subject-matter of cause or matter.

excluded but not if they are of great value and it is reasonable to believe that they have been bought with the purpose of frustrating a judgment creditor.

The order should state, preferably in a schedule, what chattels are to be seized or delivered up, and no authorization can be implied or given to enter the defendant's premises without his consent. Although the refusal of such consent is contempt of court, the plaintiff cannot insist on going into the premises, in the same way that he cannot when using an Anton Piller Order.

In *CBS United Kingdom Ltd* v. *Lambert and another*[8] the plaintiffs sought both *Mareva* and Anton Piller Orders against the defendants, together with orders for delivery up and discovery. Goulding J granted an Anton Piller Order but refused the other relief. The evidence was that the first defendant was spending considerable sums of money on easily convertible items such as motor-cars and other valuable movables, and he claimed to be unemployed. In the circumstances, the evidence seemed to point both to the first defendant arranging his affairs in order to defeat any judgment later given against him, and to the money he was using having come from the profits of infringing the plaintiff's copyright, and so the Court of Appeal granted the *Mareva*, together with an order for delivery up and discovery.

In very limited circumstances, within the spirit of the guidelines set out above, an order for delivery up will be made if the plaintiff can discharge the heavy burden of showing that it is appropriate. Further, the position of third parties in whose possession, custody or control the chattels are must be carefully considered.[9]

The pursuit of further information

In the type of case where a *Mareva* is appropriate the defendant and his colleagues or advisers will usually have

---

[8] [1983] 1 Ch 37, CA.
[9] As in *Z Ltd* v. *A-Z and AA-LL* [1982] 1 Lloyd's Rep. 240.

information vital to the plaintiff, whether to aid his case generally or to enable the *Mareva* Order to be effective.

In the ordinary way a party can seek an order for discovery relating to any matter in question in the cause between the parties.[10] However, this can only apply to cases where writs have been issued,[11] and where the discovery is to do with the issues in dispute. If the discovery is to establish what assets the defendant holds, an application under the Rules is not the correct course, but the court nevertheless has power under its inherent jurisdiction[12] to make an order in support of a *Mareva*, for example that a defendant discloses on affidavit his assets. The reason is that without such an order the *Mareva* itself might be ineffective because it does not bite on sufficient assets as these have been skilfully hidden from the plaintiff. Also, the plaintiff may be deterred from seeking or continuing a *Mareva* if he does not know how much the defendant has in case his undertaking as to damages is called upon if the order has the effect of freezing all assets in the absence of disclosure, over and above the sum necessary. This could occur, for example, if the defendant has £1 million equally in five banks, but the individual sums are not known to the plaintiff. If the *Mareva* sum is £300,000 and each bank is served with the order, the defendant's total sum of £1 million will be frozen because each bank will fear being in breach as to its £200,000. An order to disclose this information will enable release of the balance of £700,000 for the defendant's use. Similar problems can occur with other assets, and this order for discovery is frequently granted.

It should be noted that such an order is not to be used to police the *Mareva* to see if there has been a breach. Its purpose is to make effective the order by establishing the

---

[10] Order 24 generally; see Order 26 for power to order interrogatories to be answered; servants and agents of corporations can be required to give discovery on behalf of the corporation—*Anderson* v. *Bank of British Columbia* (1876) 2 Ch D 644, at p. 659; *Harrington* v. *North London Polytechnic* [1984] 1 WLR 1293, CA, at p. 1300.

[11] Preferably where pleadings have been served—*RHM Foods Ltd* v. *Bovril Ltd* [1982] 1 WLR 661, CA.

[12] *A and another* v. *C and others* [1981] 1 QB 956, Goff J.

defendant's assets. Ackner L J in *AJ Bekhor & Co Ltd* v. *Bilton* said[13]:

> ... the power to order discovery to ensure that the *Mareva* jurisdiction is properly exercised and thereby to secure its objective of preventing the defendant removing his assets from the jurisdiction and so stultifying any judgment given by the court in the action, cannot be found in the Rules ...

It may be arguable therefore whether this power is one ancillary to the *Mareva* or based on a "separate" inherent jurisdiction. In any event, it is accepted as exercisable, albeit with caution because it extends the court's interference with a party who has not yet been judged to be in breach of any legal duty.

A further basis on which to seek information is by means of a tracing order where there is a proprietary claim to assets. The purpose of this order is to search for particular funds or other assets, and not just to seek a defendant's general property. The power to make an order to trace what are essentially trust funds is well established, but because of its ramifications for third parties as well as defendants it is also exercised with caution. The reasoning for these orders was succinctly put by Templeman L J in *Mediterranea Raffineria Siciliana Petroli SpA* v. *Mabanaft GmbH*[14]:

> A court of equity has never hesitated to use the strongest powers to protect and preserve a trust fund in interlocutory proceedings on the basis that, if the trust fund disappears by the time the action comes to trial, equity will have been invoked in vain. That is why orders of this sort were made long before the recent orders for discovery, and they are at the heart of the Chancery Division's concern, and it is the concern of any court of equity, to see that the stable door is locked before the horse has gone.

[13] [1981] 1 QB 923 at p. 940; the better way to ensure compliance with a *Mareva* is to seek an order that the defendant be cross-examined on his affidavits, under Order 38, r.2, or that any variations permitted thus far be revoked, see pp. 944–5.

[14] 1978 CAT 816 (1 Dec. 1978)—money was paid by mistake to the wrong parties; *London & County Securities* v. *Caplan* (unreported) (26 May 1978)— allegations of embezzlement of £5 million.

In *Banker's Trust Co* v. *Shapira and others*[15] the plaintiff New York bank had sought to recover money paid out on allegedly forged cheques. A *Mareva* injunction was granted against assets in this country, but an order that the third defendant bank in London disclose documents relevant to the deposit of money by the first and second defendants was refused. Amongst other documents the plaintiff wished to inspect and take copies of all correspondence between the first two defendants and the bank, cheques drawn on the accounts, and all transfer applications and debit vouchers. On appeal, it was held that in these particular circumstances the order was appropriate. The normal confidentiality between a banker and his customer could not apply when there are good grounds for believing the money sought to be traced belongs to the plaintiff, because he has in equity a right to follow the money through its journey until it is found. Thus, the only effective way to protect equitable rights is to allow the plaintiff to have as much information as is relevant. The jurisdiction to grant orders for discovery in tracing operations and pure *Marevas* is similar, but clearly based on different grounds.

What is the situation where a defendant claims that he should not disclose any information because of the risk of self-incrimination? In essence, the courts are reluctant to refuse orders for this reason. In *Khan (MK)* v. *Khan (IA) and others*[16] the plaintiff gave three blank cheques with the alleged intention that the first defendant was to purchase a property for him. The sum of £40,000 was cashed but not used for the intended purpose, and after a demand for the money by the plaintiff the defendant claimed that the money was a loan. The plaintiff sought a *Mareva*, an account and inquiry, and a tracing order, and Stuart Smith J ordered the defendants to swear affidavits as to the whereabouts of the money. The defendants applied for discharge or a variation because of the risk of self-incrimination, but Wolf J dismissed their application. On appeal, it was held

[15] [1980] 1 WLR 1274, CA (4 June 1980), Lord Denning MR, Waller and Dunn L JJ; *Chase-Manhattan Bank NA* v. *Israel-British Bank (London) Ltd* [1981] Ch 105.
[16] [1982] 1 WLR 513, CA.

that the possible offences were within the exception to privilege of section 31 of the Theft Act 1968, and further, the criminal offences depended on how and why the money was used, and not where the money now was, which was the purpose of the order. Thus, a restrictive view of any privilege was taken.[17]

It is also open to one party to apply to inspect the banking accounts and records of another party under section 7 of the Bankers' Books Evidence Act 1879, which allows the court to make an order permitting any party to a legal proceeding to inspect and take copies of entries in a banker's books, so long as the inspection is in furtherance of the proceedings.[18] The Act applies to all records held by the bank in furtherance of its banking business and thus microfilm records, magnetic tapes and other mechanical and electronic data retrieval systems are included.[19] However, it is likely that most, if not all, bank correspondence is not within the phrase "bankers' books", unless it is of a specific nature relating to the mechanics of the account.[20]

The power of the courts under this Act is considerable, and cannot be used as a fishing expedition. Good, sound reasons have to exist before an application will be approved. As Lord Widgery CJ explained in *Williams and others* v. *Summerfield*[21]:

> One must . . . recognize that an order under section 7 can be a very serious interference with the liberty of the subject. It can be a gross invasion of privacy; it is an order which clearly must only be made after the most careful thought and on the clearest grounds.

An application can be made *ex parte*, but it is preferable

---

[17] Note section 72 of the Supreme Court Act 1981, reducing the scope of privilege against self-incrimination in intellectual property cases.

[18] The Act (s.10) applies to both civil and criminal proceedings; *R* v. *Kingham* [1908] 2 KB 949.

[19] *Barker* v. *Wilson* (1980) 70 Cr App R 283; Bankruptcy Act 1919, Sched. 6, para. 1; Civil Evidence Act 1968, s.5; *R* v. *Grossman* [1981] Crim LR 396—order to inspect Manx bank records refused; see also *Power Curber International Ltd* v. *National Bank of Kuwait SAK* [1981] 1 WLR 1233, CA.

[20] *R* v. *Dodson* (1973) 77 Cr App R 91.

[21] [1972] 2 QB 513, DC, at p. 518.

for notice to be given.[22] There can in fact be few circumstances that warrant an *ex parte* order, especially as it relates to documents and information maintained by the bank, and not the customer. If there is a fear that money will be removed the proper course is to apply in the first place for a *Mareva*. The Act cannot be used as a means to discover facts on which to base a *Mareva* unless legal proceedings have already started and the order is sought in connection with those. In such a case, evidence of risk which results from an order allowing inspection of accounts must, it is submitted, be relevant and admissible for a *Mareva* injunction in the same proceedings.

It has to be emphasized that information obtained by any order of the court is confidential, and cannot be used in other proceedings without leave, nor published. This is so whether the information has been read out in court or not, except that comment on it is permitted unless the court orders otherwise. In *Home Office* v. *Harman* Lord Diplock said[23]:

> ... an order for production of documents to a solicitor on behalf of a party to civil litigation is made upon the implied undertaking given by the solicitor personally to the court (of which he is an officer) that he himself will not use or allow the documents or copies of them to be used for any collateral or ulterior purpose of his own, his client or anyone else; and any breach of that implied undertaking is a contempt of court by the solicitor himself.

Security for costs

The defendant on a claim or the plaintiff on a counterclaim can ask for security for costs from the other party,[24] and the court has a wide discretion[25] to order such security when it

---

[22] See generally *R* v. *Marlborough St Stipendiary Magistrate, ex parte Simpson and others* (1980) 70 Cr App R 291, DC.

[23] [1983] 1 AC 280, HL, at p. 230; see *Customs and Excise Commissioners* v. *AE Hamlin & Co* [1984] 1 WLR 509, Ch D, Falconer J.

[24] Order 23; Companies Act 1948, s.447 for corporations.

[25] *Sir Lindsay Parkinson & Co Ltd* v. *Triplan Ltd* [1973] QB 609, CA, especially Lord Denning MR at pp. 626–7.

is just to do so, having regard to all the circumstances. In particular, the residence of a plaintiff outside the jurisdiction is important, as is the giving of a wrong address, or a deliberate change of address during the proceedings, because the aim of the order is to protect one party against the unenforceability of an order for costs against the other.

The court takes into account the plaintiff's case, and the defendant's reaction to it, and although the discretion is often exercised by ordering a payment into court or the production of a bond or guarantee, security is not often ordered in *Mareva* cases because of the tests to be satisfied before the injunction is granted. Nevertheless, in a proper case the burden is on the plaintiff to show that he has assets to satisfy any order for costs as well as his undertaking in damages, if the case goes against him.

The plaintiff can seek security against a defendant's counterclaim but his *Mareva* against the defendant will be taken into account, so that in a case where the defendant's assets within the jurisdiction and subject to a *Mareva* are enough to cover likely costs, no security will be ordered for a counterclaim despite the fact that the plaintiff's costs and his claim exceed the defendant's assets.[26] It is also unlikely that security will be granted in international arbitration proceedings, despite a *Mareva* order, when the hearing is conducted under a full and comprehensive set of provisions such as the ICC Rules.[27]

RSC Order 11[28]

The ordinary way to apply for leave to issue and serve process out of the jurisdiction is to prepare the proposed writ or originating summons with an affidavit in support for consideration by a judge in the Commercial Court or a Master elsewhere in the Queen's Bench Division.[29]

[26] *Hitachi Shipbuilding & Eng Co Ltd* v. *Viafel Compania Naviera SA* [1981] 2 Lloyd's Rep. 158.
[27] *Bank Mellat* v. *Helliniki Techniki SA* [1984] QB 291, CA.
[28] See above p. 26 *et seq.*
[29] Similar practice in other courts and other divisions of the High Court in London; leave is also necessary to serve notice of motion out of the jurisdiction in arbitration matters under Order 73.

When a *Mareva* is involved it is best to have the Order 11 application heard by the judge at the same time, especially as the *Mareva* must be based on some cause of action within the jurisdiction, so that Order 11 is often a precondition. Thus, one composite affidavit for both the *Mareva* and the Order 11 leave can be presented, together with the appropriate draft orders. Alternatively, if there is no *Mareva* application at that stage, the Order 11 application can take place in the Commercial Court without an oral hearing, by leaving the writ or originating summons, together with a draft order and the affidavit, at Room 198 (Commercial Court Listing Office), at the Royal Courts of Justice. After due consideration by a commercial judge the application will be granted or refused, and the papers marked accordingly. Note that the commercial judge may not consider the case is properly one for the Commercial Court and can therefore adjourn the application to be heard by a Master.[30] In other courts an Order 11 application is heard in the usual way, but note that if an injunction is sought at the same time a judge has to hear the application.

Judgment in default: RSC Order 13

In an action where the defendant fails to give notice of intention to defend the plaintiff can, in an ordinary case where no *Mareva* or similar order is involved, prove service of the writ by affidavit (if there is no acknowledgment of service) and enter judgment for the sum claimed, or interlocutory judgment with damages to be assed.[31] This is not possible under the Rules where a *Mareva* has been granted,[32] but it is within the inherent jurisdiction of the court to grant leave, in appropriate cases, to a plaintiff to enter judgment in default of the defendant's appearance, that is, his notice of intention to defend.[33] Further, the *Mareva* can be continued despite the judgment, so that the restraining

---

[30] Order 72, r.4(4).
[31] Order 13, rr. 1, 2.
[32] Order 13, r.6.
[33] *Stewart Chartering Ltd* v. *C & O Managements SA* [1980] 1 WLR 460; the plaintiff must show that a search for the notice of intention to defend is negative.

order stays in force until execution. The alternative would leave a loophole in the *Mareva* jurisdiction, and the policy behind the court granting leave is that it has inherent jurisdiction to control its own process and prevent any possible abuse. This jurisdiction is regularly exercised as most *Mareva* cases proceed to judgment without the appearance of the defendant.

RSC Order 14

The plaintiff in an action where a *Mareva* has been granted can serve an Order 14 summons for summary judgment once the statement or points of claim have been served, and a notice of intention to defend the action has been filed.[34] If there has been no acknowledgment of service nor notice of intention to defend, the proper course is to proceed under Order 13, above, for judgment in default. If the defendant begins to defend the action, however, a summons can be served, either returnable at the same time as a hearing to discharge or vary the *Mareva*, which means the issues can be argued conveniently at the same time, or at another time. The listing officer should be informed that the hearing will deal with more than one application if the summonses are issued at different times.

The Order 14 summons, together with an affidavit deposing to the plaintiff's belief that there is no defence and briefly outlining the facts, should be served 10 clear days before the return day,[35] although the court has discretion to hear a summons regardless. Nevertheless, adequate time must be granted to a defendant to enable him to show why summary judgment should not be granted, and dispensation with the minimum time period is not usual.

Mareva cases are often disposed of in this way, but leave to defend can be given either conditionally or unconditionally, so that a payment in has to be made or security

---

[34] Order 14, r.1(1); see notes in the *Supreme Court Practice* generally.
[35] Order 14, r.2(3).

provided before the defence is allowed to proceed, for example in cases where the defence is shadowy.[36] *Marevas* and summary judgment go hand in hand, but straightforward debt-collecting Order 14 applications are best not heard in the Commercial Court unless they are of a true commercial nature, or a *Mareva* is required at the outset, because there is little benefit in going to the Commercial Court except on the grounds of greater experience in assessing *Mareva* applications. Indeed, cases not suitable for retention in the Commercial List will be transferred out.[37]

The timely use of Order 14 is an important ancillary tactic in pursuing a defendant already subject to a *Mareva* injunction.

---

[36] Order 14, r.4; *Paclantic Financing Co Inc* v. *Moscow Narodny Bank Ltd* [1984] 1 WLR 930, CA; *Rosengrens* v. *Safe Deposit Centres* [1984] 1 WLR 1334, CA; *First City Development Corp* v. *Stevenson Construction Co* (1983) 48 BCLR 242.

[37] Order 72, r.6.

CHAPTER 9

Contempt of court

Disobedience of an injunction, whether it is a mandatory or prohibitory order, is a contempt of court.[1] Thus, refusal to comply with a *Mareva* injunction, an Anton Piller Order, or any other similar order granted by a court is contempt, for which the contemnor can be punished by an unlimited fine, and/or up to two years' imprisonment. A security for future good behaviour can also be ordered. The purpose of this power is to protect the administration of justice against abuse, and to prevent persons from deliberately ignoring the orders of the English courts.[2]

Breach of an undertaking to the court is also contempt,[3] whether it has been given in place of, or to avoid, an injunction, or otherwise, and it can be punished just as severely. This is because it is common practice for an undertaking to replace an injunction, and any other treatment of a breach would mean that an undertaking to the court was regarded as something of a lesser quality than an order by the court.[4]

What is the consequence of this rule for our purposes? First, the question of damages for a contempt should be

---

[1] *Seaward* v. *Paterson* [1897] 1 Ch 545, CA; *Martin* v. *Bannister* (1879) 4 QBD 491; Contempt of Court Act 1981; Order 52, rr.1 and 4; Order 45, rr.4, 5, 6, and 7; it is no defence to say that obeying the court order would have necessitated a breach of contract with another party—*Acrow (Automation) Ltd* v. *Rex Chainbelt Inc* [1971] 1 WLR 1676. An English court order is a good defence to an English action for breach of contract.

[2] Breach of an *in rem* arrest of a ship is also contempt, see *The Jarlinn* [1965] 3 All ER 36.

[3] The undertaking has to be given and recorded in court—*Neath Canal Co* v. *Ynisarwed Resalven Colliery Co* (1875) 10 Ch App 450; *Millburn* v. *Newton Colliery Ltd* (1908) 52 SJ 317; *Gandolfo* v. *Gandolfo* [1981] QB 359; see Chapter 4 for further discussions on undertakings.

[4] *Biba Ltd* v. *Stratford Investments Ltd* [1973] Ch 281, where a negative undertaking was given by the directors of a company not to infringe a registered trademark. It was held that a director could be committed for contempt if he was in breach of the undertaking—see especially Brightman J at p. 287.

considered. In the ordinary way, if an injunction orders a
person to refrain from a breach of contract, or from commit-
ting a tort, the act which is in contempt of the order would
also be in breach of the defendant's legal obligations, so that
the other party could sue under the appropriate head of
damage. There is, however, no right for a person to sue a
contemnor for damages for the contempt *per se*, because the
breach is of the court's order, and not of a personal right of
the other party.[5]

The courts look to the seriousness of the act in relation to
the administration of justice and its protection, and therefore decide how to punish the contempt on the basis of how
it affects the court's objective view of a particular situation.
There is no civil right to damages, and no power for the
court to award compensation for the contemnor's actions to
the other party.[6] Thus, because the *Mareva* injunction
orders a person not to do something which is itself quite
legal (in most circumstances), that is deal with his assets
as he chooses, the contemnor will usually incur no civil liability to the other party by ignoring the court order or undertaking. A court can only punish him as appropriate for his
breach of duty to the court itself. The same result will occur
for most similar orders, because there will not be an independent right to sue, for example, if a party refuses to disclose his internal management accounts, despite being
ordered to do so.[7]

In general, the *Mareva* and other orders will be served on
all relevant parties, but a person is still in contempt even
if the notice has not been served on him, with or without
the formal penal notice warning attached, so long as he
knew of the order.[8] The court equally has an "undoubted"
jurisdiction to commit a person for contempt, even if he was
not included in the order, nor a party to the action, if know-
ing of the injunction he nevertheless aids and abets a person

[5] *In Re Hudson, Hudson* v. *Hudson* [1966] Ch 209; the same applies
whether on breach of an order or an undertaking.
[6] *Chapman* v. *Honig* [1963] 2 QB 502.
[7] See Chapter 8 for the orders which are available, and their effect.
[8] *Hassan* v. *Hassan* [1962] 1 WLR 1434.

to commit a breach.[9] There is also no need to serve someone with a copy of an order of the court referring to his voluntary undertaking, before he can be committed for a breach of it.[10] The essence is knowledge, and not technical notice.

Procedure

The plaintiff who knows of a breach of the order or undertaking can, if he wishes, ask the court for an order of committal. This is the way he enforces the defendant's obligations to the court, and it is rare for a court to move of its own accord towards committal.[11]

A notice of motion, together with an affidavit in support, must be served on the alleged contemnor,[12] clearly specifying the breaches which are the basis of the motion to commit.[13] In addition to an order of committal, a writ of sequestration can be issued against the property of the contemnor, or where appropriate the property of a director or other officer of a limited company.[14] Although the plaintiff gains nothing himself by the committal, it is common in most circumstances for him to be awarded costs on a full indemnity basis.

Most moves for contempt are made to the High Court as the court originally granting the order, or receiving the

[9] *Seaward* v. *Paterson* [1897] 1 Ch 545, North J.

[10] *D* v. *A & Co* [1900] 1 Ch 484.

[11] See, however, *Clarke and others* v. *Chadburn and others* [1985] 1 WLR 78 (Ch D), Sir Robert Megarry V-C, at p. 83, where it was observed that the courts might feel it necessary to relax their present restraint on enforcing their own orders when these were openly flouted, and the administration of justices was thereby brought into disrepute; in *Attorney-General* v. *Times Newspapers Ltd* [1974] AC 273, Lord Diplock at p. 308: ". . . no sufficient public interest is served by punishing the offender if the only person for whose benefit the order was made chooses not to insist on its enforcement". The judicial response in any one instance can only depend on the particular facts as seen in the light of public policy.

[12] Order 52, r.4; in exceptional cases the order for committal can be made on an *ex parte* application, but this is usually where violence is feared.

[13] *Chanel Ltd* v. *FGM Cosmetics Ltd* [1981] FSR 471; ". . . if the plaintiff company wished to proceed it must get its tackle in order and serve a notice of motion that complied with the rules", *per* Cumming-Bruce L J, in *Jelson (Estates) Ltd* v. *Harvey* [1983] 1 WLR 1401, CA at p. 1407.

[14] Order 45, r.5.

undertaking, but it is also appropriate to make formal application to the High Court if the breach is of an order made on appeal.[15] It is nevertheless occasionally the fact that breach of, or delay in implementing, an undertaking given to the Court of Appeal demands an explanation to the Court of Appeal itself, and it is probable that the court could, of its own volition, commit a person for contempt.

Policy

Committal or a fine for contempt is the only effective way to enforce *Mareva* and other related orders. Although the funds may, for example, have been dissipated, the threat of committal is necessary to ensure that the purpose of the orders is not nullified. Committal thus acts as a deterrent and as punishment. The court must ask itself whether it is to punish alone, or to do so with the aim of enforcing the original order. In *Danchevsky* v. *Danchevsky*,[16] Lord Denning MR said[17]: "Whenever there is a reasonable alternative available instead of committal to prison, that alternative must be taken."

In the context of the *Mareva*, the alternative is in the nature of a fine, and the protection of civil justice administration may well have to be balanced against the reduction in assets of the contemnor. Would it serve the interests of justice if the court levied a heavy fine on the defendant for contempt? Yet, the court would surely consider that its primary task was to punish the breach of its order, rather than protect the plaintiff's position on judgment, although that was the reason for obtaining a *Mareva* in the first place. In fact, no record exists of a committal for contempt in respect of a breach of a *Mareva*, although motions for contempt are occasionally served for breach of Anton Piller Orders.[18]

[15] Or to the County Court if on appeal from there—*Pott* v. *Stutely* [1935] WN 140; *Fortescue* v. *McKeown* [1914] 1 Ir R 30.

[16] [1975] Fam 17, CA.

[17] At p. 22; note also Buckley L J at p. 22, E–F and Scarman L J at p. 24, D.

[18] There are more opportunities to breach a mandatory order compared to a prohibitory one.

It is also clear from the court's practice that if there is little likelihood that imprisonment will make a person comply with the order or otherwise serve a coercive purpose, he will be released once he has been sufficiently punished for the original breach.[19] The nature of a *Mareva* makes it unlikely that imprisonment will ensure compliance if the contemnor is determined to resist, but it would be correct in extreme circumstances. If the contemnor is left in prison for some time, however, the Official Solicitor will intervene, as can be seen from *Enfield London Borough Council* v. *Mahoney*.[20] The facts were that an ancient lead cross, thought to be either the "Glastonbury cross" or a copy of it, was the subject of an order by Taylor J that the defendant should deliver it up to the plaintiff local authority, on whose land it had been found. The defendant refused to hand over the cross, and the local authority moved to have him committed for contempt. As a result of his continued refusal, Croom-Johnson J committed him to prison for two years in April 1982.

The Official Solicitor, as part of his duties,[21] applied in December 1982 for the defendant's release. The application was heard by the same judge in January 1983, but adjourned. In April 1983 the defendant still refused to comply with the court order, and the application to free him was dismissed with costs against the Official Solicitor. On appeal, it was confirmed that although the Contempt of Court Act 1981 provided for a fixed term of imprisonment to be stated, the court nevertheless retained its inherent power to release a contemnor before the term had expired, regardless of whether the contempt had been purged or not. In the circumstances it was thought that the defendant had already been sufficiently punished, and no coercive effect could be expected from continued imprisonment because he would not move for his own release, and seemed to enjoy the publicity.

[19] *In re Burrell Enterprises* [1973] 1 WLR 19, CA; *Enfield London Borough Council* v. *Mahoney* [1983] 1 WLR 749, CA.

[20] [1983] 1 WLR 749, CA.

[21] Based on a direction of Viscount Dilhorne LC, 20 May 1963, which stated that the Official Solicitor will review the cases of imprisoned contemnors, and report on them quarterly.

Further, the role of the Official Solicitor was explained,
and the fact that he should be free to bring contempt cases
to the notice of the courts was relevant in looking at the
order for costs against him. As such an order might inhibit
his functions, and in the absence of impropriety on his part,
or a lack of justification for the move to release a contemnor,
no such order should be made. The case clearly confirms[22]
that committal to prison for civil contempt is first to punish
the contemnor for his disobedience to the court, and, secondly, to try to coerce him to comply with the original order
in the future.

Unjustified orders and committal

It is no defence to contempt proceedings to allege that the
order should not have been made, or has been discharged.
An order of the court must be obeyed while it stands, and a
breach is still contempt even if, at a later stage, the order
is in fact discharged.[23] The same principle applies if the
original order was wrongly made; the defendant's remedy
is to apply for its immediate discharge while keeping to its
terms.

In *Isaacs* v. *Robertson*[24] it was advised that the Court of
Appeal of St Vincent and The Grenadines was correct in
holding that an order made by a court of unlimited jurisdiction must be obeyed unless and until it is set aside. Thus it
was no excuse for a party to plead as a defence to a motion
to commit for contempt that the order was irregular. The
proper course was to apply to set it aside. As Romer L J said
in *Hadhuison* v. *Hadhuison*[25]:

[22] *Per* Watkins L J at p. 756, and *per* May L J at p. 757.
[23] *The Eastern Trust Co* v. *McKenzie, Mann & Co Ltd* [1915] AC 750, PC;
in the same way, a voluntary undertaking can only be discharged or obeyed
(not varied)—see *Cutler* v. *Wandsworth Stadium Ltd* (1945) 172 LT 207, CA;
breach of the undertaking is contempt even if the other party is prepared to
agree to the particular action. It is not up to one party to "permit" the
other to break his obligation to the court; but the circumstances of the case
will be considered by the court before deciding on punishment.
[24] [1984] 3 WLR 705, PC.
[25] [1952] P 285, at p. 288.

It is the plain and unqualified obligation of every person against, or in respect of whom, an order is made by a court of competent jurisdiction, to obey it unless and until that order is discharged. The uncompromising nature of this obligation is shown by the fact that it extends even to cases where the person affected by an order believes it to be irregular or even void.

A regular order should be the subject of an appeal to a higher court. An application to set aside an irregular order should be made to the court which granted it, and then if necessary an appeal can take place against that decision.

The use of documents and contempt

It is a general principle that documents which are disclosed by one party to another as part of legal proceedings, for example as a result of discovery, must not be used by the recipient party for any improper purpose. There is an implied undertaking on the recipient's part to obey this rule, breach of which is a contempt of court.[26] Therefore, leave of the court is necessary for any use of such documents in any other proceedings.[27] It is a rule viewed purposively, as can be seen by the fact that it applies to both documents themselves, and their derived contents, so that use of the information as against the document itself is still a breach.[28]

Contempt and the County Court

The County Court judge has, as may be expected, full and ample power to deal with contempt.[29] The present basis of

[26] *Home Office* v. *Harman* [1983] 1 AC 280, HL.
[27] See *Riddick* v. *Thames Board Mills Ltd* [1977] QB 881 (especially pp. 896 and 901); *Halcon Int Inc* v. *Shell Transport & Trading Co* [1979] RPC 97 (especially pp. 109 and 121).
[28] See *Sybron Corp* v. *Barclays Bank PLC* [1984] 3 WLR 1055, Scott J, especially pp. 1065–1070, where it was explained, *inter alia*, that a narrow interpretation would make the rule worthless.
[29] *Jennison* v. *Baker* [1972] 2 QB 52, CA—at p. 61 Salmon L J said: "The power exists to ensure that justice shall be done"; *Martin* v. *Bannister* (1879) 4 QBD 212 (DC) and 491 (CA).

the jurisdiction is contained in the County Courts Act 1984[30] and the County Court Rules.[31] An appeal against a County Court contempt order lies to the Court of Appeal direct.[32]

The effect of *Peart* v. *Stewart*,[33] where the House of Lords classified the County Court as an inferior court for contempt purposes, and so limited its power to order imprisonment to one month, has been reversed by the County Courts (Penalties for Contempt) Act 1983, which makes the County Court a superior court for contempt, and therefore able to punish on the same basis as the High Court, unless otherwise provided.[34]

Successors in title and contempt

Can a successor in title be liable for contempt of court? When an order is served on an individual who is party to the action or otherwise, his liability is clear because he is the party served. When a limited company or other corporate body is involved the position is less clear. Directors and officers of the company who are served with the order are in contempt if they breach it, and it is likely that all persons who succeed to a responsible position in the company are bound in the same way as their predecessors in office. The same principle would make a successor company taking over the business liable if the order was applicable to them, but the problem is that an injunction is relief *in personam*. For our purposes though, the likely situation is that a question of staff change will arise, and it should be straightforward to show that, for example, the new managing director of a company is as liable for breach of an order by the company as his predecessor who was actually served with the

---

[30] Section 38—jurisdiction for the injunction; s.118—committal for contempt in court and similar, *R* v. *Lefroy* (1873) LR 8 QB 134.

[31] Order 29; Service of the order is necessary (r.1(2)), and there must be a penal notice as to the effect of a contempt (r.1(3))—*Iberian Trust Ltd* v. *Founders Trust & Investment Co Ltd* [1932] 2 KB 87; *Hampden* v. *Wallis* (1884) 26 Ch D 746.

[32] Administration of Justice Act 1960, s.13.

[33] [1983] 2 WLR 451, HL.

[34] Section 1 provides a new subsection (4A) to s.14 of the Contempt of Court Act 1981.

order.[35] It can perhaps safely be assumed that both a company and its officers are bound to obey an order of the court or comply with an undertaking even if there is a change of personnel during the course of the proceedings. Any other view would be open to justified criticism.[36] It is nevertheless always possible for an applicant for a *Mareva* or other order to draft it in such a way as to include all future servants and agents, if it is considered appropriate to do so on the facts of the case.

Z Ltd v. A-Z and AA-LL[37]

The greater part of the judgment of Eveleigh L J in this case was concerned with the contempt aspect of *Marevas*, especially as it affected banks and third parties.[38]

In essence, a third party is liable if he knowingly assists in the breach of the injunction or, to put it another way, he is in contempt if he knows of the terms of the injunction but nevertheless wilfully assists in a breach by the person to whom it was addressed. Indeed, it is clear that the third party is in contempt even if, for example, the defendant has not yet received notice of the injunction, because the contempt is not simply the aiding and abetting of a contemnor, but the third party's own and personal interference with the administration of justice.

The position is more complicated when dealing with a financial institution such as a bank, with separate departments and large numbers of employees. How far are all employees bound, and is the bank responsible for their actions? Naturally, the employer is responsible for the employee if he knowingly assists in the breach of a court order during the course of his employment.[39] However, what

---

[35] See generally *Re British Concrete Pipe Association* [1983] ICR 215; *Heatons Transport (St Helens) Ltd* v. *T&GWU* [1973] AC 15, HL; *Z Ltd* v. *A-Z and AA-LL* [1982] 1 QB 558, CA, at p. 580.
[36] There are some USA cases, e.g. *Lucy* v. *Adams* 224 F Supp 79.
[37] [1982] 1 QB 558, CA, Lord Denning MR, Eveleigh and Kerr L JJ.
[38] *Ibid*, at pp. 578–583.
[39] *Ibid*, at p. 581, D.

if the employee does not know of the order, and unintentionally disobeys it, even though another employee has had notice? Eveleigh L J stated[40]:

> The position could be said to depend upon the status of the person receiving the notice and the relationship between him and the person making the payment. In my opinion, however, in all cases it should be necessary to show that the person to whom notice was given authorized the payment or, knowing that the payment was likely to be made under a general authority derived from him, deliberately refrained from taking any steps to prevent it. I do not think that it should be possible to add together the innocent state of mind of two or more servants of the corporation in order to produce guilty knowledge on the part of the corporation.

Further, it was later said[41]:

> ... It will obviously be prudent and in its own interests for the bank to take some steps in the matter. If it does nothing and a cheque is cashed or some other transaction completed, the bank may find it difficult to resist an inference that there was complicity in or connivance at the breach. It will be a question of fact and degree in every case. The greater the difficulty in discovering the account and consequently controlling it, the less likely the risk of contempt of court.

Therefore the applicant for a *Mareva* must make certain that the order is clear as to its scope and the involvment of the bank. The order will usually refer to numbered accounts, but it is better to be as specific as possible in all respects, especially where the order indicates a maximum sum, because then the bank has freedom to pay if the assets exceed the figure in the order. The bank could be caught between breach of contract with its customer on the excess sum, and contempt of court if a payment is made when the actual amount still held is less than the maximum sum. The banks are in such a difficult position that Eveleigh L J went on to add that[42]:

> Carelessness or even recklessness on the part of the banks ought not in my opinion to make them liable for contempt

[40] *Ibid*, at p. 581, E–F.
[41] *Ibid*, at p. 582, F.
[42] *Ibid*, at p. 583, E.

unless it can be shown that there was indifference to such a degree that was contumacious. A *Mareva* injunction is granted for the benefit of an individual litigant and it seems to me to be undesirable that those who are not immediate parties should be in danger of being held in contempt of court unless they can be shown to have been contumacious. This is a matter which should be borne in mind when the judge is asked to make the order. The more information he possesses, the more specific he can be and where it is possible to designate a particular account which is the subject of the order, and this whether general or a maximum sum order, the account will naturally be specified.

These are welcome guidelines for banks and others, and indeed quite generous to the banks. It is clearly necessary to prove guilty knowledge on their part, and in the light of general business administration, perhaps that is all that can be done for something as serious as contempt. The bank often has existing arrangements with others which will be safeguarded by these guidelines, such as the cheque-card scheme. In the same way that a bank guarantees to honour a cheque even though funds are insufficient, so long as there is a cheque-card arrangement relied upon, so too can it seemingly debit the customer's account, despite the *Mareva*, when the same circumstances exist. Although there is a £50 limit on such payments, the principle is one which may overreach into other arrangements, and is therefore of potential far beyond its immediate application. This view will have to be balanced against the rule that liability to others is not generally any defence to contempt proceedings, as was discussed above.

In the light of this case the position of banks and third parties is now much clearer. There must, for contempt, be *mens rea* with knowledge of the effect of the action, regardless of whether the contemnor is a party to the legal proceedings, or has been served personally with the order or notice of it.

The undertaking to issue a writ

A failure to issue a writ expeditiously when an undertaking to do so[43] has been given to the court is a contempt of court

---

[43] See also Chapter 4.

by the plaintiff, even though he employs legal advisers to take care of his litigation. This principle has been reinforced by *PS Refson & Co Ltd* v. *Saggers and another*,[44] where writs in three cases were issued 16, 18 and 19 days after the undertaking was given. Nourse J was moved to make his declaration in the absence of any complaint by the defendants involved because this breach of an undertaking is serious, and merited special attention. It was emphasized that a solicitor's failure to issue a writ on the intended plaintiff's behalf is aiding and abetting the contempt, a breach of his duty to the court, and makes him liable to be reported to The Law Society.[45]

The civil consequences of contempt

It was discussed above that a plaintiff, for example, who moves to commit a defendant for contempt, has no claim against him for the contempt *per se*. Nor does the plaintiff have the right, because of the contempt, to apply to set aside any disposition that has been made. Thus, the sale of assets by the defendant to a third party, whether at an undervalue or not, against the terms of a *Mareva*, is a contempt of court, but the third party will *prima facie* get good title. The fact that the sale is in direct contravention of a court order does not invalidate it. This is consistent with the right of a bona fide purchaser for value without notice to get good title despite any defect in the "seller's" title.[46] As the defendant to a *Mareva* still owns his assets,[47] a third party cannot, under ordinary sale of goods principles, be in a worse position on purchase from him than from someone not the owner. What if the third party knew of the contempt? The defendant would still be the owner of the goods, but should knowledge of the breach invalidate the sale? At present, no such power is exercised by the courts, although it would be a highly effective way of enforcing the public policy of

[44] [1984] 1 WLR 1025 (Ch D), Nourse J.
[45] See *R&T Thew Ltd* v. *Reeves (No 2) Note* [1982] QB 1283.
[46] The exception to the *nemo dat quod non habet* rule; see also ss.21–26 of the Sale of Goods Act 1979.
[47] Subject to possible exceptions where title is in dispute.

contempt proceedings, and ensuring even greater success for the *Mareva* injunction. As Sir Robert Megarry V-C has said[48]: ". . . (it) may be no bad thing if to the recognised remedies available for breach of an order of the court there comes to be added a power to declare invalid acts done contrary to the order."

This new power would be consistent with avoiding acts in fraudulent preference on bankruptcy and liquidation, and could be most appropriate where there was a lack of good faith on the part of the buyer, and/or clear notice of the contempt, or sale at an obvious undervalue sufficient to put a reasonable purchaser on notice.

For the present, if some equitable right in the property itself could be alleged, and some notice of that right could be shown, perhaps a *Mareva* should be applied for against the third party who could not show himself to be a bona fide purchaser for value without notice, to preserve the assets pending final resolution of the main claim. This would be an extension of the *Mareva*, but a limited and justifiable one when exercised against third parties in contempt of the original order, or against purchasers with knowledge of the whole circumstances of the sale or transfer.

---

[48] *Clarke and others* v. *Chadburn and others* [1985] 1 WLR 78, Ch D at p. 82; see the discussion above at p. 18 for an example of how the Family Division deals with reviewable dispositions.

CHAPTER 10

The "Mareva" in private international law

The development of the *Mareva* in broadly English disputes is bound to influence its use in international litigation or arbitration. In one fundamental respect this has already been achieved through the Civil Jurisdiction and Judgments Act 1982 and the consequent acceptance for the United Kingdom of the principles of the 1968 Brussels Convention on jurisdiction, and recognition and enforcement of judgments. This is a significant change, and integrates in a practical manner the dispute-resolution processes in member States.

The potential use of the *Mareva* and other interim relief goes much further, however. Although a work of this size cannot deal adequately with the full impact of private international law on the jurisdiction and procedure of the English courts,[1] several points merit attention because of their potential benefit, and the questions they raise.

Concurrent overseas proceedings

First, the extension of *Mareva* orders to more situations within the field of private international law is a logical progression, given the history of the injunction so far. If the aim of just and convenient relief is maintained, together with the increasing willingness of the English courts to

---

[1] Reference should be made to the standard works on the subject, especially Dicey and Morris, *The Conflict of Laws*; Cheshire and North, *Private International Law*.

recognize the jurisdiction of foreign courts and overseas arbitral tribunals, the *Mareva* will become of greater use, especially as its use in England is a question for English law as the *lex fori*, because a *Mareva* is essentially a matter of procedural, rather than substantive, law. Thus it is for the English courts and the United Kingdom Parliament to regulate its application, and there is little evident reluctance to employ the *Mareva* when circumstances demand, subject only to a fundamental objection based on jurisdiction.

One possible extension is therefore in the type of case where proceedings are possible in more than one jurisdiction, including England. If the litigation starts in England, and is accepted as being within this jurisdiction, and there are assets here which could be the subject of a *Mareva*, is the opportunity of seeking such an order lost if the courts later stay the English proceedings in favour of an action in another jurisdiction?

For example, the defendant may successfully argue that there is a foreign jurisdiction clause,[2] or the principles of *lis alibi pendens*[3] apply, or indeed a combination of these principles expressed in the view that the foreign jurisdiction is more convenient. Can the court nevertheless grant the plaintiff a *Mareva* to preserve assets in England pending the outcome of the foreign proceedings? This would give the plaintiff assets against which he would seek to enforce the foreign judgment,[4] and such an order would be a co-operative action in line with comity, albeit without statutory provision, and a departure from existing practice. In effect, however, it is the same as the new provisions of the Civil Jurisdiction and Judgments Act 1982 as to interim relief in England when action is being taken in a Convention country. So long as the order staying the English proceedings is expressed in terms which do not preclude the grant of a *Mareva*, and so long as jurisdiction itself is not challenged

---

[2] See *The Fehmarn* [1958] 1 WLR 159; *The Eleftheria* [1970] P 94.
[3] See *The Christianborg* (1885) 10 PD 141; *The Atlantic Star* [1974] AC 436; *MacShannon* v. *Rockware Glass Ltd* [1978] AC 795; *Castanho* v. *Brown & Root Ltd* [1981] AC 557; *The Abidin Daver* [1984] AC 398, HL.
[4] See later p. 119.

successfully, there is nothing inconsistent with a *Mareva* injunction in England when foreign litigation is undertaken. After all, the English court does not declare itself to be incompetent by granting the stay, but instead defers to another court for any number of sound and practical reasons.[5] The English jurisdiction is not renounced but stayed, and therefore the applicant for a *Mareva* in such circumstances could still show, first, that the English courts had jurisdiction, secondly, that he had a good arguable claim, and, thirdly, that there were assets here.

The same reasoning would allow a defendant here to apply for a *Mareva* against the plaintiff's assets pending the outcome of the foreign litigation, either for a counterclaim or for costs, even though it is his application to stay the English proceedings. The position should be no different if the plaintiff here is the defendant abroad. Once the jurisdictional test[6] is satisfied it is a question of discretion, and in many instances a *Mareva* here to guard against an empty judgment from another jurisdiction would be an appropriate exercise of that discretion. Needless to say, if the English courts decide that a foreign court has exclusive jurisdiction, there could be no *Mareva* here, except under the 1968 Convention, for which see below.

Overseas divorces and matrimonial proceedings

Another area of change is in the recognition of overseas divorces.[7] One anomaly which arises with regard to some cases, especially of *talaq* divorces, is that financial relief on dissolution is not available, or generally not granted, in the overseas jurisdiction, and despite the existence of assets in this country the English courts were powerless to grant any relief because they did not have jurisdiction in the main

---

[5] See generally *The Abidin Daver* [1984] AC 398, HL.

[6] *The Siskina* [1979] AC 210, HL; and Chapter 3 p. 30.

[7] Now basically under the Recognition of Divorces and Legal Separations Act 1971, implementing the essential provisions of the 1968 Convention of the Hague Conference on Private International Law.

proceedings.[8] Of course, many jurisdictions allow some financial relief in the form of maintenance or periodical payments, at least for the children, which could be enforced here under a variety of statutes and agreements,[9] but the main problems arise more frequently now because of the greater number and increased mobility of married couples from jurisdictions where a marriage can be dissolved with comparative ease, and without current provisions for financial relief.

This can have unfortunate consequences for the divorced party,[10] especially as the statutory rights of occupation under the Matrimonial Homes Act 1983 end on divorce. Short of challenging the overseas divorce[11] and seeking a decree here,[12] which would involve considerable difficulties, the respondent could claim an interest in the former matrimonial home by way of equitable relief,[13] or she might apply for maintenance of the children if she gains custody of them.[14] She might also attempt an application under section 17 of the Married Women's Property Act 1882. A *Mareva* is appropriate in all such cases where there is a risk of dissipation of assets, and it is submitted that a legal or equitable claim in England, combined with assets here, in these cases would be enough to permit the court to grant one. This is especially useful because of the basic restriction of section 37 of the Matrimonial Causes Act 1973 to cases where the main matrimonial proceedings are, or were, in England.[15]

---

[8] Dicey and Morris, Rule 50; Matrimonial Causes Act 1973, ss.22, 23, 24, 27 and 31; the Domestic Proceedings and Magistrates Courts Act 1978 does not apply to respondents outside the EEC.

[9] E.g. the Maintenance Orders (Facilities for Enforcement) Act 1920, but this is of limited use, especially as it does not apply to Pakistan. Note also the new Maintenance Orders (Reciprocal Enforcement) Act 1972.

[10] See *Quazi* v. *Quazi* [1980] AC 744, HL; *Torok* v. *Torok* [1973] 1 WLR 1066.

[11] Under, e.g. s.8(2) of the Recognition of Divorces and Legal Separations Act 1971; *Newmarch* v. *Newmarch* [1978] Fam 79.

[12] See Matrimonial Causes Act 1973 generally.

[13] See e.g. *Eves* v. *Eves* [1975] 1 WLR 1338 CA; *Hussey* v. *Palmer* [1972] 1 WLR 1286, CA; *Cooke* v. *Head* [1972] 1 WLR 518, CA.

[14] Guardianship of Minors Act 1971, s.9; Matrimonial Causes Act 1973, s.23(2)(*b*).

[15] See Chapter 4 p. 42, and Chapter 2 p. 17.

Further relief is planned under the Matrimonial and Family Proceedings Act 1984[16] which will allow financial relief to be granted in England after an overseas divorce by judicial or other means. This covers the extra-judicial divorce of *talaq*, and grants a right to the divorced party to claim through the English courts on a similar basis to a party divorced here. There are powers akin to section 37 of the Matrimonial Causes Act 1973 to restrain a party from taking action to defeat a claim, regardless of whether the court has yet granted leave for an action or not.[17] This might be thought to exclude the *Mareva* in practice, but in the same way that the flexibility of a *Mareva* or similar order can be of advantage in purely English proceedings,[18] so too can the use of a *Mareva* in these overseas cases be a benefit, especially when speed is needed.[19]

Although the sums at stake are inconsequential in comparison to the more common commercial *Marevas*, the benefit to individual litigants is potentially much greater. There is also clearly a need for protection, and the opportunity for self-help can only reduce the cost to the community at large.

Foreign judgments and awards

A judgment creditor with a foreign judgment debt in his favour can no longer sue here on the original cause of action.[20] He has, however, a range of options to enforce the judgment in England, including summary proceedings under RSC Order 14, or registration under statute and consequent enforcement and execution[21] as a judgment of the English courts.

[16] Part III (ss.12–27), not yet in force.
[17] Section 23 and s.24 of the Matrimonial and Family Proceedings Act 1984.
[18] See Chapter 4 p. 42.
[19] Section 23(9) and s.24(3) state that the powers are without prejudice to s.37 of the Supreme Court Act 1981.
[20] Section 34 of the Civil Jurisdiction and Judgments Act 1982.
[21] Including therefore powers under s.138 of the Supreme Court Act 1981; Charging Orders Act 1979; Order 45, rr. 3 and 4; Order 47; Order 49; Order 51. See also Order 71; Order 14, rr.3–20; Dicey and Morris, Rules 181–189; and the cases referred to in Chapter 11, p. 133, concerning the enforcement of an English judgment in favour of BP Exploration against Mr Hunt.

Order 14 is the appropriate course for liquidated claims with little or no defence, and in general terms a foreign judgment fits in to this category because the issue between the parties has been joined and decided, and the judgment is often for a definite sum of money, including costs. Thus, so long as it is not a penal[22] or revenue judgment, and is final and conclusive, it can be enforced through the Order 14 procedure, and a *Mareva* injunction is available to preserve assets here pending execution. The new Order 11 specifically provides for issue and service of a writ out of the jurisdiction for claims on "any judgment or arbitral award".[23]

Alternatively, discretionary registration under the Administration of Justice Act 1920[24] is possible, or mandatory registration under the Foreign Judgments (Reciprocal Enforcement) Act 1933.[25] In the former case a judgment creditor can still sue on the judgment, but because he chooses not to use the simpler procedure of registration he will not usually get his costs. In the latter case he can only register, and has no separate right of action on the foreign judgment.[26] Thus, a party seeking to apply for a *Mareva* to protect assets pending execution could easily do so if he is suing on the judgment debt, but may have difficulty in persuading a court that it has jurisdiction to grant a *Mareva* before registration because there is, in the case of the 1933 Act, no legal action pending or possible. Once the judgment has been registered, however, a *Mareva* can be granted to preserve assets pending execution, in the usual way.[27] It can be argued that the right of registration of a judgment is a legal right which should be protected when it is just and convenient to do so, even before the registration has taken place.

---

[22] Mixed civil and criminal judgments can be enforced as to the civil part—*Raulin* v. *Fischer* [1911] 2 KB 93.

[23] Order 11, r.1(1)(*m*); see fn. 34 below, and the BP Exploration cases referred to in fn. 21 above, together with *Perry* v. *Zissis* [1977] 1 Lloyd's Rep. 607, CA.

[24] Section 9.   [25] Sections 2, 12 and 13.   [26] Section 6.

[27] Simon Brown J granted a *Mareva* in aid of execution of a Kenyan judgment (registered under the Administration of Justice Act 1920) on 18 April 1985.

When the foreign judgment is from one of the EEC countries, enforcement again takes place through registration,[28] and no action is possible on the judgment itself.[29] However, in these cases a *Mareva* or some other interim relief in England is possible before judgment, under the reciprocal provisions of the 1968 Brussels Convention (discussed below), and this relief can be continued after judgment in aid of execution.

Arbitral awards

A person with a foreign award in his favour can ask the courts of the place of arbitration to declare the award enforceable there, or otherwise obtain a judgment on it, and enforce the court order here[30] by action or registration, as discussed above.

A much more straightforward procedure is to enforce the award by registration under Part II of the Arbitration Act 1950,[31] or under the Arbitration Act 1975,[32] or under other statutory provisions,[33] which all have the effect of enforcing the award under section 26 of the Arbitration Act 1950, when it will be executed as a judgment of the English courts. Alternatively, an action on the award may be started in the same way as on a foreign judgment debt, but with the added advantage that because the award necessarily arises out of a voluntary submission to arbitration as a means of resolving the

[28] Section 4 of the Civil Jurisdiction and Judgments Act 1982, and Article 31(2) of the Convention; UK judgments are enforced under s.18 of the Civil Jurisdiction and Judgments Act 1982.

[29] *De Wolf* v. *Cox*, Case 42/76, [1976] ECR 1759.

[30] *East India Trading Co Inc* v. *Carmel Exporters & Importers Ltd* [1952] 2 QB 439; and see *Union Nationale des Cooperatives Agricoles* v. *Catterall* [1959] 2 QB 44; *International Alltex Corp* v. *Lawler Creations Ltd* [1965] IR 264; Order 73, r.8; Dicey and Morris, Rules 202–204.

[31] Based on the 1927 Geneva Convention for the Execution of Foreign Arbitral Awards.

[32] Based on the 1958 New York Convention on the Recognition and Enforcement of Foreign Arbitral Awards.

[33] Section 18 of the Civil Jurisdiction and Judgments Act 1982 for UK awards; some awards will come within the Administration of Justice Act 1920, the Foreign Judgments (Reciprocal Enforcement) Act 1933, and the Arbitration (International Investments Disputes) Act 1966.

dispute, it is thus more clearly a debt arising out of a contractual obligation, and less open to challenge.

A *Mareva* is equally permissible to preserve the defendant's assets pending execution of an award, and if the defendant is not within the jurisdiction, nor has submitted to it, leave under Order 11 can be sought for issue and service of the writ.[34]

Consequently, the *Mareva* is a valid and potentially useful order to ensure the practical mobility of foreign judgments and awards, and to make real the purpose behind the principles that have developed as to their recognition and enforcement. If there is any difficulty seeking a *Mareva* when an immediate cause of action is not clear because, for example, of the administrative provisions as to registration, it is submitted that a claim for a declaration could be made, or an undertaking given to issue process for such a declaration, so that the *Mareva* can be attached to a specific action before the courts, and thus sought in compliance with the established guidelines and rules.[35]

The 1968 Brussels Convention[36]

As part of the harmonization procedures of the EEC, a Convention on the jurisdiction of courts, and the recognition and enforcement of judgments in civil and commercial cases, was agreed in 1968 and came into force in 1973; an Accession Convention was signed in 1978 to cover the new membership of the United Kingdom, Denmark and Ireland.

The Civil Jurisdiction and Judgments Act 1982 sets out the new law necessary to make sense of the Conventions, and the first four Articles provide the most immediate change in English law:

[34] Under Order 11, r.1(1)(*m*); see fn. 23 above.
[35] Especially Order 29, r.1; see Chapter 3 at p. 30, and Chapter 4 at p. 33; the right to have the judgment or award enforced should be sufficient.
[36] The following discussion can only be a brief one with regard to *Mareva* and similar orders. For a full view of the new law see the Civil Jurisdiction and Judgments Act 1982, the Jenard Report (OJ 1979 No C59, p. 1), the Schlosser Report (OJ 1979 No C59 p. 71), Collins, *The Civil Jurisdiction & Judgments Act 1982*, Hartley, *Civil Jurisdiction and Judgments*.

Article 1—This Convention shall apply in civil and commercial matters whatever the nature of the court or tribunal. It shall not extend, in particular, to revenue, customs or administrative matters.

The Convention shall not apply to:
(1) the status or legal capacity of natural persons, rights in property arising out of a matrimonial relationship, wills and succession;
(2) bankruptcy, proceedings relating to the winding-up of insolvent companies or other legal persons, judicial arrangements, compositions and analogous proceedings;
(3) social security;
(4) arbitration.

Article 2—Subject to the provisions of this Convention, persons domiciled in a Contracting State shall, whatever their nationality, be sued in the courts of that State. Persons who are not nationals of the State in which they are domiciled shall be governed by the rules of jurisdiction applicable to nationals of that State.

Article 3—Persons domiciled in a Contracting State may be sued in the courts of another Contracting State only by virtue of the rules set out in Sections 2 to 6 of this Title.

In particular the following provisions shall not be applicable as against them:
... in the United Kingdom—the rules which enable jurisdiction to be founded on:
(a) the document instituting the proceedinggs having been served on the defendant during his temporary presence in the United Kingdom.

Article 3 also excludes other examples of exorbitant jurisdiction, discussed in Chapter 11, and the rules in sections 2 to 6 referred to cover special jurisdiction, insurance, consumer contracts, exclusive and chosen jurisdiction. Article 4 makes it clear that defendants not domiciled in a Contracting State nevertheless have the same rights as the law of that State gives them, but a plaintiff who is domiciled in a Contracting State can sue them under the ordinary rules of jurisdiction, unhampered by the exclusion of an exorbitant jurisdiction.

The different rules available for jurisdiction[37] when a person can be sued in another Contracting State apart from

---

[37] Article 5.

the one he is domiciled in are important, and these include the right to sue a defendant in the place of performance of a contract,[38] the right to pursue a maintenance creditor where he is habitually resident, the right to sue in tort where the harmful act occurred, and the jurisdiction of a court to hear a counterclaim. Other rules apply to trusts, branches and agencies, co-defendants, third parties, and joint civil and criminal cases.

Further, there is exclusive jurisdiction for the *lex situs* where immovable property is concerned, if the proceedings are to do with rights *in rem* or tenancies, and the courts of the place where a company has its seat have exclusive jurisdiction for the validity of a company's constitution, and its nullity or dissolution, except when winding up for insolvency.

Amongst the wide and far-reaching provisions is the one vital to our discussion, allowing protective measures to be taken by any Contracting country if there are proceedings in another Contracting State.

Article 24 sets out the basic power as follows:

> Application may be made to the courts of a Contracting State for such provisional, including protective, measures as may be available under the law of that State, even if, under this Convention, the courts of another Contracting State have jurisdiction as to the substance of the matter.

Section 24 of the Civil Jurisdiction and Judgments Act 1982 clarifies the position as to interim relief pending the trial or an appeal, and allows the English court jurisdiction to grant relief even if the subject-matter of the continuing proceedings is a question of jurisdiction, or a reference to the European Court under the 1971 Protocol to the 1968 Convention.

Section 25 of the same Act reverses the effect of *The Siskina*[39] for Convention countries, and provides:

> (1) The High Court in England and Wales or Northern Ireland shall have power to grant interim relief where—
> (a) proceedings have been or are to be commenced in a Contracting State other than the United Kingdom or in a

---

[38] *De Bloos* v. *Bouyer*, Case 14/76, [1976] ECR 1497; *Tessili* v. *Dunlop*, Case 12/76 [1976] ECR 1473; *Ivenel* v. *Schwab*, Case 133/81 [1982] ECR 1891.
[39] [1979] AC 210, HL.

> part of the United Kingdom other than that in which
> the High Court in question exercises jurisdiction; and
> (b) they are or will be proceedings whose subject-matter is
> within the scope of the 1968 Convention as determined
> by Article 1 (whether or not the Convention has effect
> in relation to the proceedings).
> (2) On an application for any interim relief under subsection
> (1) the court may refuse to grant that relief if, in the opinion
> of the court, the fact that the court has no jurisdiction apart
> from this section in relation to the subject-matter of the pro-
> ceedings in question makes it inexpedient for the court to
> grant it.

Subsection (3) provides for an Order in Council extending
the power and jurisdiction of interim relief not only to countries other than Contracting States, but also to proceedings
whose subject-matter is not within Article 1, as set out
above, and to arbitration proceedings (see Chapter 4). The
use of such an extension would be appropriate in many
instances, not least for Commonwealth cases where the
system of law has retained recognizable links with English
law. As discussed above, the growing use of the *Mareva* can
only lead to a more international dimension, and section 25
is thus of powerful potential.

At present, when the standard provisions of the Act are
fully in force, a plaintiff suing in, for example, France, can
apply to the English courts to freeze the defendant's assets
in England, provided the Convention applies to the original
claim.[40] Once a foreign judgment has been given in France,
he can enforce his judgment debt against the defendant's
assets here, under the recognition and enforcement procedures of the Convention.[41] There is thus complete interac-
tion between the Member States on the principle that a
party's assets may be frozen in one way or another pending
the outcome of a trial.[42] However, as these extended powers
only apply to matters within the Convention, interim relief
in other cases will still depend for the moment on those

[40] See Article 1, and *W* v. *H*, Case 25/81 [1982] ECR 1189.
[41] See fn. 29 above; s.4 of the Civil Jurisdiction and Judgments Act 1982;
Article 31(2) of the Convention.
[42] See Chapter 11 for a comparative view of the available measures.

parallel provisions of English law as are unaffected by the Conventions themselves.

There have been occasions when the scope of the main Convention has been criticized as unclear, and one such case was *De Cavel* v. *De Cavel (No 1)*.[43] The question was whether the proceedings were to do with rights in property arising out of a matrimonial relationship, and thus excluded by Article 1, or not. The judgment of the European Court of Justice made it plain that property rights between spouses were not necessarily excluded from the Convention, but only if they were contingent on divorce or other matrimonial proceedings. The European Court also said:

> As provisional protective measures relating to property—such as the affixing of seals or the freezing of assets—can serve to safeguard a variety of rights, their inclusion in the scope of the Convention is determined not by their own nature but by the nature of rights which they serve to protect.

It must be considered, though, that the reciprocal enforcement and recognition of judgments does not include the enforcement of protective measures. Thus, the *saisie conservatoire* of a French court will not be enforced in Germany[44] or any other Convention country. The plaintiff in France will have to apply for the relief available in the appropriate country, for example in England he can seek a *Mareva* Order, if he wishes to protect his position so far as assets outside France are concerned. The existence of Article 24 is a guide to the direction such a plaintiff should take when searching for assets and deciding how to preserve them.

---

[43] Case 143/78 [1979] ECR 1055.
[44] *Denilauler* v. *Couchet*, Case 125/79 [1980] ECR 1553; the very nature of provisional and protective measures makes them outside the Convention because the guarantees of notice and service of documents inherent in the almost automatic recognition and enforcement of *inter partes* hearings are not present. It is therefore up to each jurisdiction to demand its own guarantees from an applicant for interim relief before granting an order; see also Article 27 (grounds for non-recognition), Article 31 (enforcement), Articles 46 and 47 (service of documents).

CHAPTER 11

A comparative view of "Mareva" and similar orders

The *Mareva* injunction itself is, as a matter of procedure, a part of the *lex fori* in England and therefore will be governed by English law whatever the *lex causae* of the underlying dispute. As a procedural matter, foreign law has no direct influence on the *Mareva*, despite its possible effect on the substantive issues, but it is nevertheless interesting to note the use of interim preservative orders in other jurisdictions, especially in the Commonwealth, the United States of America, and the EEC countries. Given the statutory basis of the *Mareva* injunction, it is not proposed to consider whether the *Mareva* is a rebirth of either traditional common law principles or of the old law merchant.[1] Its importance is as a judicial response to the facts of particular situations, and therefore the examples of statutory and judicial protection of parties in other jurisdictions is more relevant to an overall understanding of the *Mareva* concept.

[1] Lord Denning MR referred to the old process of foreign attachment in the City of London in *Pertamina* [1978] 1 QB 644, CA, at pp. 657–658; see also Lawton L J in *The Siskina* [1979] AC 210, at p. 236, and in *Third Chandris Shipping Corporation* v. *Unimarine SA* [1979] 1 QB 645, CA at p. 670; *Mayor of London* v. *Cox* (1867) LR 2 HL 239 (Willes J), *Tapp* v. *Jones* (1874) LR 9 CPD 418, and *Mayor of London* v. *London Joint Stock Bank Ltd* (1881) 6 App Cas 393, HL, contain relevant points on the old procedures. The latter case decided that foreign attachment was a personal remedy (not applicable against a corporation) and had to be strictly pursued according to custom. It is unlikely that foreign attachment in England was not abolished by the late 19th century in the Common Law Procedure Acts of 1852, 1854 and 1860. (See further Bohun, *Privilegia Londini* (1723), and Pulling, *The Laws, Customs, Usages and Regulations of the City and Port of London* (1842)).

Europe

The French practice of *saisie conservatoire* has frequently been compared to the *Mareva* injunction,[2] and it is contained in the French Code of Civil Procedure.[3]

Article 48 provides that in cases of urgency, where recovery of the debt appears to be in peril, a creditor with an apparently valid claim can seek authorization from the court to attach (*saisir conservatoirement*) movables belonging to the alleged debtor. The creditor is given a certain time within which to start an action to support his claim, and he can be required to put up security, or otherwise prove his solvency, in case of an adverse judgment against him. The *saisie conservatoire* can be varied or discharged on application by the debtor if there are serious and legitimate reasons to do so, or alternatively on deposit with a receiver appointed by the court of the sum claimed.[4]

Further, a creditor can seek leave to register a pledge or charge (*inscription de nantissement*) against a debtor's business assets (*fonds de commerce*),[5] and a judicial mortgage (*hypothèque judiciaire*) against a debtor's immovable property.[6] These powers are exercisable by the president of the *tribunal de grande instance*, or the *juge d'instance*,[7] or the president of the *tribunal de commerce*,[8] depending on the subject-matter and value of the claim. The significance of the orders is their effect on the property attached, and it

[2] E.g. Lord Denning MR in *Pertamina* [1978] 1 QB 644, at p. 682, C and Orr L J at p. 664, C, and Sir John Donaldson MR in *Tracomin SA* v. *Sudan Oil Seeds Ltd* [1983] 1 WLR 1026, CA at p. 1033, G.

[3] *Ancien Code*, Articles 48–57 as amended (based on Law of 12 November 1955); these provisions are specifically unaffected by the new Code of Civil Procedure—Article 50 of this latter code provides that interlocutory matters (*incidents d'instance*) are to be generally decided in the court where the action is tried. Note that the exorbitant jurisdiction of the French courts whereby foreigners can be summonsed to answer for obligations contracted towards Frenchmen (Article 14), and Frenchmen can be summonsed for any obligations in or out of France (Article 15) does not apply to Convention States under Article 3 of the 1968 Convention.

[4] Article 50.
[5] Article 53.
[6] Article 54.
[7] Article 48.
[8] Article 56.

expresses the attitude of French law that in general terms a debtor's property is the common pledge of his creditors. In comparison with the *Mareva*, the *saisie conservatoire* gives the creditor actual rights in the property and is, therefore, a means of enforcing security and preserving assets for the particular creditor's claim, rather than generally.

The powers are equally applicable on general principles when an arbitration award has been given in France because it is enforceable on the basis of *res judicata* (or *force de la chose jugée*). A foreign award is similarly entitled to be used as a claim for security if it is both recognizable and enforceable, as it is then an apparently well-founded debt within Article 48.

Belgium, as may be expected, has similar provisions in its procedural law,[9] as does Italy.[10] In Switzerland procedural matters are dealt with on a cantonal basis, but the principles of *saisie conservatoire* are known and understood in most areas.[11]

In West Germany the code of Civil Procedure, or *Zivilprozessordnung/ZPO* of 30 January 1877 provides for protection of a judgment creditor or plaintiff against an empty judgment by either allowing the attachment of assets belonging to the potential judgment debtor,[12] or by granting an interim order[13] to preserve the status quo pending litigation. Attachment is often made conditional on the plaintiff putting up security in case his claim is later dismissed, and the defendant in his turn can furnish security to have the order revoked. He can also apply to the court for a direction that the plaintiff must start his main claim within a certain time, and if this is not complied with the attachment

[9] Contained in the Belgian Code of Civil Procedure; also Article 1298 (*saisi-arrêt* and third parties) Civil Code; note *Morgan* v. *Vve Lauritz-Lund* Cass Belg (17 November 1897) Pas Belge 1989 I 21.
[10] Known as *procedimenti cautelari*; there must be evidence of a risk, and the likelihood of a favourable judgment in the main action; see Articles 670 *et seq.* of the Italian Code of Procedure.
[11] E.g. in Geneva; some cantons do not permit attachment if the defendant is resident or domiciled in Switzerland, or in the canton itself.
[12] Known as *Arrest*, under s.916 *et seq.*, ZPO; there must be a good claim (*Arrestanspuch*) and reason to fear an empty judgment (*Arrestgrund*).
[13] Known as *Einstweilige Verfügung*, under s.936 *et seq.*, ZPO.

is revoked automatically.[14] Both the *Amtsgericht* and the *Landgericht*[15] have jurisdiction in cases within their statutes, and applications are frequently based on documents alone.

The exorbitant jurisdiction of the German courts whereby claims are heard if a defendant owns assets in Germany,[16] regardless of any other connection, cannot be exercised for claims within the Brussels Convention of 1968.[17]

Sweden, as an example of a Scandinavian country, also has interim protective measures in its Procedural Code.[18] Attachment (*kvarstad*) can be ordered if there are good grounds for a claim, and it is reasonably expected that the other party will abscond, remove his assets, or otherwise evade his obligation to pay his debts,[19] or if there is a risk that property subject to a claim will be removed, will substantially deteriorate, or be used to the detriment of the applicant's position.[20] Further, an injunction can be granted to stop actions which would affect a party's legal rights.[21]

An applicant for any of these orders has to provide security for damages in case his claim is unfounded, and although a temporary *ex parte* attachment order is common, the full documents in the case have to be served soon after the original order has been made. The applicant must also start his litigation or arbitration reference within one month of the attachment. The putting up of security by the defendant entitles him to have the order automatically discharged.

Thus it can be seen that orders similar to, and often more powerful than, *Marevas* are available in leading European jurisdictions. What is the situation in other common law countries?

The USA

The right of foreign attachment is a familiar concept in the USA.[22] At one time it was generally used to seize or attach

[14] Section 726, ZPO.
[15] Equivalent in broad terms to a Small Claims Court (under DM 3,000), and a District Court respectively.
[16] The notorious s.23, ZPO.
[17] See Article 3 of the Convention.
[18] In Chapter 15 of the Code ("RB").
[19] RB 15.1
[20] RB 15.2
[21] RB 15.3
[22] E.g. Lord Denning MR in *Pertamina* [1978] 1 QB 644, at p. 658, D–F.

property belonging to non-residents or absconding debtors, probably based on the customs of England before the settlement of the American colonies, but it did not appear to have been usually allowed for unliquidated claims or where equitable relief was sought.

It is doubtful whether, looking at reported United States cases as a whole, the powers of foreign attachment can be said to be similar to the *Mareva*, or even in common use today. One foremost factor in foreign attachment is to compel the appearance of the absent defendant, and the order has the effect of an *in rem* or quasi *in rem* action, whereby the property seized can be used to satisfy the plaintiff's claim.[23] In some States, therefore, the attachment can give a lien on the property to enable the plaintiff to execute a judgment against it.[24] Most States provide for the plaintiff to show some evidence of a risk of dissipation, in addition to the defendant being absent or a non-resident, and also some good reason why the claim should be heard.[25] It is generally necessary for the plaintiff to provide security for damages in case the attachment is later found to have been unjustified. Judgments obtained on the basis of this *in rem* or quasi *in rem* procedure are rarely enforced in other States, despite the Full Faith and Credit Clause in the American Constitution which provides that competent courts in one State are entitled to have their judgments recognized by the courts of another State.[26]

It is submitted that the practice of the United States' courts in this area is of little assistance in considering the *Mareva* injunction. The aim of foreign attachment seems to be as much to claim jurisdiction[27] as to preserve the assets

[23] See *Harris* v. *Balk* (1905) 198 US 218; *Ownby* v. *Morgan* (1921) 256 US 94 (especially Pitney J at p. 104); *De Beers Consolidated Mines Ltd* v. *United States* (1945) 325 US 212.
[24] *Percy Ross* v. *Peck Iron & Metal Co Inc*, 264 Fed 262.
[25] *Shaffer* v. *Heitner* (1977) 433 US 186; 97 SC 2569.
[26] *Pennayer* v. *Neff* (1877) 95 US 714.
[27] Much like the doctrine of arrestment *ad fundandam jurisdictionem* in Scotland (not applicable to Convention countries under Article 3)—see *Alexander Ward & Co Ltd* v. *Samyang Navigation Co* [1975] 1 WLR 673, HL, especially Lord Kilbrandon at pp. 685–686; *Longworth* v. *Hope* (1865) 3 M 1049.

of the defendant for the plaintiff, and the lien or charge on the property seized is contrary to the *Mareva* principles.

The Far East

The courts in Malaysia regularly grant *Mareva*-type orders. The first reported case to deal with the subject was *Zainal Abidin Bin Haji Abdul Rahman* v. *Century Hotel Sdn Bhd*[28] where the facts were that the plaintiff had agreed with the defendents to rent a floor in their hotel, to be used as a recreation and leisure centre. There were disagreements between the parties about renovations the plaintiff had done, and he also feared that the hotel would be closed, thus denying him his main chance to attract customers.

The defendants were wholly owned and controlled by another company, and the plaintiff claimed that unless restrained by the court the assets of the defendants would be transferred to the controlling company and would not be available for execution of a judgment in his favour, on the main claim of a breach of contract. The High Court in Kuala Lumpur dismissed the application on the basis that it had no power to grant a *Mareva*-type order, and further that there was, in any event, no evidence of risk that the defendants' assets would be dissipated to frustrate a judgment.

On appeal, the Federal Court held that there was ample jurisdiction to grant a *Mareva* injunction,[29] but that in the circumstances of the case it was not appropriate to do so. In particular, it is interesting to note that the likely insolvency of a debtor was held not to be a base on which to build the claim for a *Mareva*. Indeed, the court said[30]: "The defendant in a suit or matter is not called upon to prove its solvency the moment it becomes a defendant and proceedings of this kind are not a means by the use of which it can be called upon to do so."

[28] [1982] 1 ML J 40 (High Court—Civil Suit, 16 October 1981); [1982] 1 ML J 260 (Federal Court—Civil Appeal, 22 January 1982).
[29] Based on para. 6 of the Schedule to the Courts of Judicature Act 1964; leading English authorities were relied on, as was the New Zealand case of *Hunt* v. *BP Exploration Co (Libya) Ltd* [1980] 1 NZLR 104.
[30] At p. 264.

Recently, the Malaysian courts have exercised their powers to preserve assets with a *Mareva* in a series of proceedings taken by the Bank Bumiputra, and Bumiputra Malaysia Finance against Encik Lorrain and others,[31] and the reports of the hearings indicate that orders for discovery were also made.

In Singapore, the court would seem to have similar powers under the Civil Law Act of 1970,[32] and the jurisdiction of the Hong Kong courts is referred to in *Chen Lee Hong-man* v. *William Chen*.[33] In Australia, the *Mareva* has been used in many cases, although doubted in some others. In New South Wales it has been held that there is no jurisdiction to grant one,[34] but a later case approved the injunction in principle.[35] In South Australia a restrictive approach has been taken,[36] but in Western Australia *Marevas* have been granted,[37] as they have been in Victoria,[38] and in Queensland.[39]

In New Zealand, too, the *Mareva* has found favour, not only in further aspects of the world-wide attempts to enforce

[31] Order granted by Mr Justice Dr Zakaria Yatin in Chambers, 10 and 15 January 1985 (*The Star; The New Straits Times*, 18 January 1985).

[32] Section 4(8); see note in [1981] 2 ML J cvii, mentioned by the Federal Court of Malaysia, see fn. 28 above.

[33] [1981] HKLR 176 (High Court of Hong Kong—Mr Commissioner Hooper); see s.19 of the Supreme Court Ordinance, equivalent to s.37 of the Supreme Court Act 1981.

[34] *Ex parte BP Exploration Co (Libya) Ltd* [1979] 2 NSWLR 406, Powell J (based on the English case of *BP Exploration Co (Libya) Ltd* [1976] 1 Lloyd's Rep. 471), claimed under s.66(4) of the Supreme Court Act 1970, but *Mareva* possible under the same Act, s.23, on the basis of jurisdiction necessary for the administration of justice; see also *Balfour-Williamson (Australia) Pty Ltd* v. *Dauterluingne* [1979] 2 NSWLR 884.

[35] *Turner* v. *Sylvestre* [1981] 2 NSWLR 295, Rogers J, where it was said at p. 305: "During the time it takes a plaintiff to obtain judgment, the defendant utilizes the time to remove all his assets from the jurisdiction. In this sense, it is said the defendant is abusing the court's process".

[36] *Pivaroff* v. *Chernabaeff and others* (1978) 16 SASR 329, Supreme Court, Bray C J.

[37] *Sanko Steamship Co Ltd* v. *DC Commodities (Australasia) Pty Ltd* [1980] WAR 51, Supreme Court, Loran SPJ (based on s.25(a) of the Supreme Court Act 1935).

[38] *Praznovsky* v. *Sablyack* [1977] VR 114, Supreme Court, Harris J (based on s.62(2) of the Supreme Court Act 1958); *JD Barry Pty Ltd* v. *M&E Construction Pty Ltd* [1978] VR 185.

[39] *Hunt* v. *BP Exploration Co (Libya) Ltd* (1980) 28 ALR 145.

the judgments in the BP Exploration litigation against Mr
Hunt,[40] but also in other reported cases.[41] The Australian
and New Zealand cases are usefully reviewed in *Riley
McKay Pty Ltd* v. *McKay*,[42] and it is clear that the modern
practice is based on the inherent jurisdiction of the courts
to regulate their administration and act to protect the interests of parties in appropriate cases.

Canada

There has also been approval for the *Mareva* in Canada,
for instance in the North West Territories in another case
connected with the BP Exploration litigation,[43] in Ontario,[44]
and through a decision of the Federal Court in *Elesguro* v.
Ssangyang Shipping Co Ltd.[45]

There can thus be little doubt that, with some exceptions
and restrictions, the *Mareva* is accepted in all major jurisdictions based on English law. It operates in the same way
as it does in England, even though its statutory base may
differ, and its effect is the same. Its almost universal welcome in these jurisdictions must underline its practical
importance and necessity.

The Middle East

The modern codes of the Arab countries of the Middle East,
based in large measure on Egypt's experience of the modern

[40] *Hunt* v. *BP Exploration Co (Libya) Ltd* [1980] 1 NZLR 104, Barker J
(based on s.16 of the Judicature Act 1908, providing all necessary power to
administer the laws of New Zealand).

[41] *Mosen* v. *Donselaar* [1980] 1 NZLR 115; *Systems & Programs (NZ) Ltd*
v. *PRC Public Management Services (Inc) and others* [1980] 1 NZLR 115.

[42] [1982] 1 NSWLR 264 (New South Wales Court of Appeal—Street CJ,
Hope JA, Rogers AJA).

[43] *BP Exploration Co (Libya) Ltd* v. *Hunt* (1980) 14 DLR (3d) 35, North
West Territories Supreme Court, Tallis J (based on s.19(*h*) of the Judicature Ordinance RP NWT 1974).

[44] *Liberty National Bank & Trust Co* v. *Atkins* (1981) 121 DLR (3d) 160,
High Court of Ontario, Montgomery J (based on s.19 of the Judicature Act
1970).

[45] (1980) 117 DLR (3d) 105.

reception and absorption of foreign law, and its amalgamation with traditional legal and customary principles, have many examples of interim preservative powers. In Egypt, these powers are contained in the Code of Civil Procedure,[46] and many other countries, especially in the Arabian Gulf, have similar provisions.[47] It is the better view that these interim powers are more akin to those of the civil law countries, rather than to the *Mareva* of the common law, but at least their existence indicates the acceptance of preservative measures in a different legal context, albeit one with a blend of traditional Islamic and modern "Western" law.

Conclusion

The *Mareva* injunction is a part of English domestic law. Consequently, the use of similar powers overseas is noteworthy, but cannot affect English practice, except to point the way where an overseas jurisdiction has developed its own *Mareva* principles further than is the case here. Certainly, there is no need to harmonize the *Mareva* with the *saisie conservatoire* of civil law countries, not only because the latter order is still an alien procedural concept, but also because the *Mareva* itself achieves its desired purpose in England, and needs no radical change to the idea of security or attachment to make it more workable.

---

[46] 1968 Articles 316 *et seq.*, based originally on Title III (Execution), and Title IV (Diverse Procedures) of the Mixed Code of Civil Procedure (1875) and the Native Code of Civil Procedure (1883), and the jurisprudence which developed in interpreting and applying these rules. The powers to grant urgent relief are now exercised in special sittings of the Summary or District Courts, depending on the dispute and the amount in issue.

[47] In addition, an embargo on travel can be ordered against a party in Saudi Arabia, and there are various other personal restrictions that can apply. Kuwait, Bahrain and Qatar recognize pretrial restraint, as does Abu Dhabi in the United Arab Emirates.

Precedents

"Mareva" Order for assets up to £100,000, including either bank accounts or assets

IN THE HIGH COURT OF JUSTICE   1985A. No.
QUEEN'S BENCH DIVISION
COMMERCIAL COURT

The Hon Mr Justice ......

Between:

A. B. TRADING LIMITED
Plaintiff

—and—

P. Q. EXPORT LIMITED
Defendant

UPON HEARING Counsel for the Plaintiff ex parte

AND UPON READING the [draft][1] affidavit of Thomas Atkins, sworn on the first day of February 1985

AND UPON the Plaintiff by its Counsel undertaking:

1. To abide by any Order this Court may make as to damages, in case this Court shall be of the opinion hereafter that the Defendant should have sustained any by reason of this Order which the Plaintiff ought to pay.

2. To indemnify any person other than the Defendant its servants or agents to whom notice of this Order is given, against any reasonable costs expenses fees or liabilities incurred by it in complying with this Order.

3. To issue forthwith and serve upon the Defendant as soon as is practicable a writ of summons in this action in

---

[1] If not sworn before the hearing an undertaking should be given, as set out after para. 3.

the form of the draft general indorsement[2] initialled by Mr. Justice——together with this Order and the affidavit referred to above.

[4. To cause the draft affidavit specified above to be sworn forthwith.]

4. To notify the Defendant of the terms of this Order as soon as is possible, by Telex or cable or courier service.

5. To notify immediately and confirm in writing the terms of this Order to any third parties affected.

IT IS ORDERED THAT

1. The Defendant, whether by itself its servants or agents or otherwise howsoever be restrained until trial or further Order from removing any of its assets out of the jurisdiction, or disposing of or charging or otherwise dealing with any of its assets except in so far as the value of such assets exceeds £100,000.

2. In particular and without prejudice to the generality of the foregoing, the Defendant whether by itself its servants or agents be restrained until trial or further Order from:

(a) drawing from, charging or otherwise dealing with any accounts standing in its name or to its order[3] at Excelsior Private Banking Corporation, Little River Street, London EC4, including account number 1515089,[4] except in so far as any of these accounts exceeds £100,000.

Provided that nothing in this Order shall prevent the said Excelsior Private Banking Corporation from exercising any right of set-off it may have in respect of any facilities it may have afforded the Defendant before the date of this Order.[5]

[2] Where the writ has neither been issued nor drawn up. Alternatively the proposed writ can be handed up to the judge.

[3] This may be too wide an order if, e.g. the bank has no means of telling whether accounts are nominee accounts or not.

[4] To be used where a specific account is confidently expected to contain the defendant's money.

[5] Proviso as suggested in *Oceanica Castelana Armadora SA of Panama* v. *Mineralimportexport (Barclays Bank International intervening), The Theotokos* [1983] 1 WLR 1294, Lloyd J.

(b) removing from the jurisdiction, disposing of or charging or otherwise dealing with any and all Oriental carpets belonging to the Defendants and/or held to their order by Acme Carpet Warehouses International, Unit 11, Heathrow Trading Estate, so as to reduce the value of the same below £100,000.

3. There be liberty to the Defendant and to any other person affected by this Order to apply on notice to the Plaintiff's solicitors to set aside or vary this Order or to seek further directions hereunder.

4. Costs be reserved.

Dated this fifth day of February 1985.

Order for Delivery up of chattels.[6]

The Defendant does forthwith upon the service of this Order deliver up or cause to be delivered up into the custody of [the Plaintiff's solicitors Messrs. Terence O'Leary & Co.] *or* [a receiver appointed by the High Court] the property specified in the Schedule below together with all documents of title relating thereto and together with the registration documents and all keys relating to the motor-vehicles therein listed.

Schedule

One painting of Paris by Moonlight, signed AR, unframed, 2'6" by 3', oils on canvas, as per attached photograph.

One Rolls-Royce Motor-Car registration number B179 ZZF, believed to be two-tone blue.

One Rolls-Royce Motor-Car registration number A179 ZZG, convertible, believed to be white.

[6] Order included in the terms of, e.g. the usual *Mareva*, following guidelines of the Court of Appeal in *CBS (UK) Ltd* v. *Lambert and another* [1983] 1 Ch 37, especially pp. 752–753.

Disclosure of Assets[7]

The Defendant does forthwith within four days of service of this Order disclose by way of affidavit served on the Plaintiff's solicitor the full value of its assets within and without[8] the jurisdiction identifying with complete particularity the nature of such assets their whereabouts and in whose possession they may be found and in whose name or to whose order they are held.

Without prejudice to the generality of the foregoing the Defendant does identify forthwith all bank or other accounts held in its name or otherwise to its order and the sums standing to such accounts.

Anton Piller Order[9]

The Defendant, whether by himself or by any person appearing to be in charge of the premises in the Schedule annexed hereto, does at any hour between 9 o'clock in the morning until 8 o'clock in the afternoon permit the person who shall serve this Order upon him together with such persons as may be duly authorized by the Plaintiff's solicitors not being more than three in number to enter each of the premises set out below and any outhouse warehouse or other building or storage area which forms part of the said premises for the purpose of inspecting photographing and seeking for and removing into the Plaintiff's solicitors' custody any material or equipment used or capable of being used or intended to be used for making illicit video tapes of the film "Flight to Tara" together with any copies of the said film and any documents relating thereto.

---

[7] See Chapter 8 for the discussion on disclosure. This draft paragraph can be inserted in the *Mareva* precedent above; the exact wording will alter depending on what precise information is sought, and what is contained in the other paragraphs of the order.

[8] Good reasons have to be advanced before a defendant is ordered to disclose his assets outside the jurisdiction.

[9] This is the operative part of the Order against an individual alleged to be making illicit videotape copies of one film.

Schedule[10]

....
....
....
....
....

AND THE COURT DECLARES[11] that in default of compliance with this Order by the Defendant or any person appearing to be in charge of the said premises the Plaintiff shall be at liberty to apply to the Court for the immediate committal to prison of any person in such default without further notice.

[10] The addresses of the premises are placed here for convenience.
[11] This notice as to contempt of court would appear after the paragraphs containing Orders; any appropriate combination of Orders is permitted depending on the relief necessary in a particular case.

Index

Official Solicitor, 105, 106
"Operation Julie", 83

Passing off, 88
Patents, 88
Payne Committee Report (on the Enforcement of Judgment Debts)
1969 (Cmnd 3909), 21
Police
applications for *Mareva*, 25n, 69, 77, 79–82
difficulties associated with *Mareva*, 82
Precedents, 137–141
Private international law, use of *Mareva* in, 115–126
Probate actions, 28
Property
immovable, 28
movable, rights over, 28
see also Assets
Purchasers for value
in receipt of good title , 62
with defect in seller's title, 112

Schlosser Report, 122n
Security
for costs, 95–96
to discharge order, 65
Set-off
of bank loans, 57, 66
to reduce *Mareva* sum, 49–50
Ships
arrest, effects of, 20
assets covered by *Mareva*, 38, 39–40
breach of *in rem* arrest, 101n
jurisdiction, 20
Singapore, measures similar to *Mareva*, 133
Sweden, measures similar to *Mareva*, 130
Switzerland, measures similar to *Mareva*, 129

Theft, 77
Third parties
adverse effects on, 11, 53
applications to clarify order, 56–57
as judgment creditors, 64–65
costs, 57
freedom to trade, 52
liability for contempt, 109
payment of debts due to, 53–54
protection of funds, 92–93
variation of order in favour of, 51–54